Twayne's United States Authors Series

Sylvia E. Bowman, *Editor*

INDIANA UNIVERSITY

Ambrose Bierce

 180

AMBROSE BIERCE

By M. E. GRENANDER
State University of New York at Albany

TWAYNE PUBLISHERS
A DIVISION OF G. K. HALL & CO., BOSTON

FOR MY COLLEAGUES

Preface

THE CRITICAL and public response to Ambrose Bierce, probably more than to any other American writer, has been curiously ambivalent. Two reasons account for what Carey McWilliams deplores as the "fugitive and elusive" reputation "of this strange, aloof, and solitary figure in American letters, so hard at first acquaintance to place or relate to his contemporaries." These factors—inadequate study of his work and misunderstanding of his life—have directed the organization of this book. For, as McWilliams succinctly points out,

the best of Bierce . . . should be part of every American's inheritance.

And so should Bierce the man. To identify him properly—he has been grotesquely misplaced—he should be thought of as somehow belonging to the same spiritual company as Justice Oliver Wendell Holmes. . . . Both fought with conspicuous gallantry in the Union Army in the Civil War, were severely wounded, and carried throughout their lives the deep, invisible scars of that tragic experience. Both were disillusioned with post-Civil-War America, adopted a frosty Olympian manner, and went in for a kind of Social Darwinism on social issues. Yet Holmes and Bierce embodied the finest elements of American idealism and each maintained, in his own way, an integrity of purpose and a fierce private patriotism that remained unaffected by the corruption of the postwar decades. Each was secretly proud of his fine military record, carried himself like the soldier he was, and used a pen like a rapier. Each had come close to death himself and had seen many fine men die; with both, an outward stoicism concealed a remarkable inner sensitivity. Both were men of great force, of acute perception, of commanding presence. At heart both were romantic idealists who, in later life, must have been troubled by echoes of the

lovely bugle calls that long years ago had summoned them to
such horrors as Cold Harbor and Shiloh. Both had learned that
in the midst of life there is always death; that in pursuit of
great dreams men stumble over cadavers and fall headlong into
pools of blood. Yet both men had moments when the searing
experiences of the Civil War were to be preferred, in retrospect,
to the degradation of that war's ideals in the decades that followed. They were immensely attractive men, handsome, debonair, erect, in the habit of looking out and over life, so to
speak, as from an eminence.[1]

This is high praise, indeed. Nevertheless, McWilliams'
thumbnail sketch is profoundly accurate. Unfortunately,
such insight is rare. The gross misunderstanding of Bierce
the man can be traced not only to the overwhelming dis-
traction of his mysterious disappearance in Mexico but to
his personal magnetism. He aroused strong emotions—positive or negative—in nearly everyone he met. Although a few
puzzled individuals attempted various ingenious theories to
account for the complexity of his character, most regarded
him as either cloven-hoofed or as sporting wings.

This spectrum of reactions has continued among the
many published interpretations, and the Bierce mythology
has grown, for the vagaries of circumstance have scattered
the primary material in a large number of repositories.
Bierce's life is undoubtedly tied intimately to his writing,
but to attempt an obvious correspondence between them
would be not only superficial but misleading. Exactly what
the relation is remains a question that can be answered
only by recourse to very deep-seated psychological mo-
tivations.

I have, accordingly, in the first six chapters of this study,
presented a straightforward biographical account, necessarily condensed. These chapters constitute no more than an
introduction, but they do rectify some prevalent errors of
fact and interpretation, and they also furnish a basis for
understanding Bierce's character. Although indebted to the
pioneering investigations of others, chiefly McWilliams, Paul
Fatout, and Napier Wilt, I have gone back, for the most
part, to primary sources. Where Bierce's writing and life
seemed mutually illuminating, I have included references to
his work. In this connection I have on occasion discussed

his letters and other personalia, his minor works as well as some of his more important ones, and his journalism. But I have kept speculation to a minimum.

A second reason for the perplexity concerning Bierce's significance is that his vast literary production has not been carefully investigated. His astounding versatility led him to write in many different forms on many different subjects. This variety and range have been difficult to cover with a single umbrella, and have precluded viable generalizations. In many cases, we have not yet developed critical concepts enabling us to deal adequately with his work. The short story, for example, in which Bierce did much of his best writing, has not yet been adequately treated in terms of esthetic theory. Nor have such short forms as the epigram, the satirical definition, and the brief fable, in all of which Bierce excelled. What we need, therefore, is not glib summary but precise study.

Consequently, I have indicated some directions for a more accurate appraisal of Bierce's writing. In Chapters 8 to 12, I have analyzed in detail some of his enormous output. My approach is intensive rather than extensive; my aim has been understanding of a limited number of works, rather than superficial coverage of everything he wrote. In these chapters I have deserted chronology entirely, basing my commentaries on the twelve-volume *Collected Works* Bierce himself revised and edited. Chapters 8 to 11 owe a great debt, acknowledged in the Notes, to the late Ronald Salmon Crane. Whether Professor Crane would have agreed with my extensions of his theories and the application I have made of them I cannot say, but my gratitude for his perception and wisdom is profound.

In the last chapter I have summarized the obstacles to an adequate appraisal of Bierce and pointed out some promising areas for future investigation. I have also noted growing signs of an intelligent appreciation of his work, both here and abroad, and have indicated his significance to American literature.

The curators of many repositories of Bierceiana have been uniformly courteous and helpful, as have private owners who have generously allowed me to examine their holdings; all these collections are listed in the Bibliography under "Primary Sources." I wish to acknowledge particularly the assistance rendered by the staffs of The Huntington Library, San Marino, California; The Bancroft Library of the University of California at Berkeley; the Division of Special Collections of Stanford University; the libraries of the University of Southern California and the University of California at Los Angeles; The Carl H. Pforzheimer Library; Yale University Library; the Clifton Waller Barrett Collection, now at the University of Virginia; the Berg Collection of The New York Public Library; Dartmouth College Library; and the National Archives.

Bierce has no living direct descendants. However, I thank the large number of his collateral descendants who have granted me permission to use unpublished material.

Financial assistance, for which I am deeply grateful, was given me by the Research Foundation of State University of New York, The Carl and Lily Pforzheimer Foundation, and the Henry E. Huntington Library and Art Gallery. I wish also to thank the State University of New York at Albany for a sabbatical leave in 1967-68. Finally, my gratitude goes to fellow members of the faculty at SUNYA for friendly assistance and encouragement.

M. E. GRENANDER

State University of New York at Albany
21 November, 1970

Contents

Chronology

1842 Ambrose Bierce born June 24 in Meigs County, Ohio. Son of a farmer and descendant of seventeenth-century New England family.

1846 Moved to northern Indiana. There he attended high school and worked on antislavery paper.

1859 Student at Kentucky Military Institute.

1860 Returned to Indiana.

1861 Enlisted for three months as private in Ninth Indiana Infantry Regiment. Engagements at Philippi, Laurel Hill, Rich Mountain, and Carrick's Ford. Mustered out in Indiana; reenlisted for three years; promoted to sergeant-major. Skirmishes at Greenbrier and Camp Allegheny.

1862 Sent to Nashville as part of Buell's Army of the Ohio. Battle of Shiloh and advance to Corinth. Commissioned second lieutenant. Battle of Stones River.

1863 Commissioned first lieutenant; acting topographical officer on staff of William B. Hazen. Battles of Chickamauga, Lookout Mountain, and Missionary Ridge. Enlistment expired. Furloughed to Indiana. Engaged to Tima Wright.

1864 Reenlisted and returned to front. Sherman's March to the Sea. Series of skirmishes and battles in Georgia. Wounded at Kenesaw Mountain; hospitalized in Chattanooga; furloughed to Elkhart, Indiana. Engagement to Tima broken. Rejoined Fourth Army Corps. Battles of Franklin and Nashville. Winter quarters in Huntsville, Alabama.

1865 Participated in Sherman's Carolinas Campaign. Demobilized late March or early April. Spring and summer worked as Treasury aide in Alabama. September took trip to Panama. Returned to New Orleans, thence to Indiana.

1866 Summer, joined Hazen in Omaha for military expedition through Indian country to San Francisco.

1867 Resigned from Hazen's expedition; secured job in Sub-Treasury at San Francisco. Breveted to major. Began training himself to be a writer. Poems and prose in the *Californian.*

1868 Essays and sketches in *The Golden Era* and the *News Letter.*

In December became editor of the *News Letter* and began writing "The Town Crier."

1871   "Grizzly Papers" and first story, "The Haunted Valley," in *The Overland Monthly*. December 25, married Mollie Day; settled in San Rafael.

1872   In March, resigned from *News Letter*; left for England with Mollie. In London, began writing for *Fun* and *Figaro* and sent letters to the San Francisco *Alta California*. Began planning first book with John Camden Hotten. Moved to Bristol. First child, a son, Day, born in December.

1873   Moved to Bath. *The Fiend's Delight* and *Nuggets and Dust*. Returned to London. Bierce family visited Paris with Mrs. Day. Returned to Bath.

1874   *Cobwebs from an Empty Skull*. Moved to Leamington. Second son, Leigh, born April 29. Wrote *The Lantern*.

1875   In April, Mollie, Day, and Leigh returned to San Francisco. Bierce moved to London. Left England in September, arriving October in San Francisco, where daughter Helen was born October 30. Got job in United States Mint.

1876   In February, father died.

1877   Associate editor of *The Argonaut*; began "Prattle." *The Dance of Death* and *Map of the Black Hills Region*.

1878   In May, mother died.

1880   General agent of the Black Hills Placer Mining Company, Rockerville, Dakota Territory.

1881-   In January, 1881, returned to San Francisco, becoming editor
1886   of the *Wasp*, continuing "Prattle" there, and writing items for *The Devil's Dictionary*.

1881-   Driven by asthma, lived at Auburn, Sunol, St. Helena,
1899   Angwin, Berkeley, Oakland, San José, Los Gatos, Wright's Station.

1887   Began writing for William Randolph Hearst's *San Francisco Examiner*, continuing "Prattle."

1888   Separation from Mollie.

1889   Day killed in gun duel over girl.

1891   *The Monk and the Hangman's Daughter* began appearing serially in the *Examiner*.

1892   *Tales of Soldiers and Civilians* published simultaneously with English edition, *In the Midst of Life*. The *Monk* appeared in book form. *Black Beetles in Amber*.

1893   Continuous squabbles with Danziger over both *Monk* and *Black Beetles*. *Can Such Things Be?*

1895- Series of articles on Spanish-American War.
1898

1896 Sent to Washington by Hearst to head lobby opposing Congressional passage of Collis Huntington's Funding Bill for Central and Southern Pacific railroads. Bill defeated, largely through Bierce's efforts. Began writing for Hearst's *New York Journal.* In November, returned to San Francisco.

1897 Series of resignations from Hearst papers, but always lured back by Hearst himself.

1898 *In the Midst of Life.*

1899 *Fantastic Fables.* In December, left for East.

1900- Except for trips, lived in Washington. Carrie Christiansen a
1913 close friend; acted as his nurse and secretary. Moved in military circles, spending much time at Army and Navy Club.

1900 On payroll of *New York Journal* ($100/week), although his material was also appearing in *New York American* and *San Francisco Examiner.* Leigh married.

1901 March 31 Leigh died.

1902 Helen married Samuel Judson Ballard. Danziger signed over all rights in *Monk* to Bierce.

1903 *Shapes of Clay.*

1905 Mollie and Ambrose divorced; Mollie died April 27. Began writing for *Cosmopolitan.*

1906 Ballards divorced. *The Cynic's Word Book.* Resigned from newspapers, but continued writing for Hearst's *Cosmopolitan,* which took over his salary.

1907 Helen married Harry D. Cowden. *The Monk and the Hangman's Daughter. A Son of the Gods and A Horseman in the Sky.*

1908 Began preparing *Collected Works.*

1909 Resigned from *Cosmopolitan. The Shadow on the Dial,* edited by Silas Orrin Howes. *Write It Right.*

1910 Summer and autumn in California.

1912 *Collected Works* completed (12 volumes). Second summer and autumn in California. Began plans for trip through Mexico to South America.

1913 Left Washington, October 2; preliminary trip through Civil War battlefields. In November, crossed border from El Paso to Juarez. From there to Chihuahua. Last letter (December 26) states that he intended to go to Ojinaga the next day.

1914 Probably killed during battle of Ojinaga, January 11.

CHAPTER 1

The Purple Fields of War

UNQUESTIONABLY Bierce's four years as a Union soldier in the Civil War were seminal. He went into the conflict a raw, half-educated teen-ager, a private filled with idealistic illusions and uncertain of his abilities. He emerged a battle-scarred officer, veteran of the Western Theater; his mettle under fire had been repeatedly tested, and his skill and courage had earned him rapid promotions and assignments to highly technical posts as topographical engineer and staff aide.

More importantly, Bierce had gained an understanding of the horrors of military carnage and a sense of comradeship with his gallant foemen of the Lost Cause. The store of reminiscences he acquired he was to use over the years for some of his finest essays and stories. And he had come to know himself: not only his strengths but the inner terrors which everyone must learn to cope with in moments of crisis to meet the recurring challenges of life.

I *Farm Boy*

On a warm, clear day, a ten-year-old farm lad, sprawled in the grass on a sunny green slope, was poring over Pope's translation of the *Iliad*. From time to time, as the wind ruffled his blond curls, he lifted blue-gray eyes from his book to survey the pastoral scene below. The boy was Ambrose Gwinnett Bierce, and the incident symbolized not only the solace he found in nature but the reading and study through which he pulled himself from "obscurity, privation and labor in the fields."[1] He was born to such a life June 24, 1842, on a small farm in southeastern Ohio. Scion of a seventeenth-century New England family whose parents had emigrated to the Middle West, Ambrose was the tenth of thirteen children and the youngest to live to maturity.

In 1846 the Bierces moved from Ohio, which was later to furnish the setting for "The Suitable Surroundings" and

15

"The Boarded Window" (*Works*, II, 350-72), to a farm in
northern Indiana. Here Ambrose grew up, finding compan-
ionship with his brother Albert, two years his senior; and
walking three miles to school in Warsaw. From the age of
fifteen to seventeen, he lived there, working as printer's
devil on the recently founded antislavery paper, *The Northern Indianan*. Then in 1859 he was sent to the Kentucky
Military Institute, to study draftsmanship, surveying, and
civil and topographical engineering. In 1860 he returned to
Indiana, where he worked on the family farm, as a laborer
in a brickyard, and as waiter *cum* handyman in a general
store and saloon. He also acquired a girl friend, Bernie
Wright, whom he called "Fatima."

II *Raw Recruit*

When the Civil War exploded, Bierce, like many another
young man, found an outlet for his talents and an opportunity for travel and adventure in the army. His firsthand
knowledge of the irrepressible conflict blazed forth, years
later, in some of the finest and most harrowing studies in
all American literature of this blood-stained era. The background on which he drew for these accounts therefore de-
serves close scrutiny.

He enlisted on April 19, 1861, as a private for three
months' service with the Ninth Indiana Infantry. This volunteer regiment arrived at Grafton, West Virginia, on June
1, joining the command of Major General George McClel-
lan. On June 3, it engaged in the putative first battle of the
Civil War, a minor skirmish at Philippi, and then camped
for five weeks in the beautiful Cheat River Mountains.

But Bierce was shortly to become a hero, in an incident
he was "vain enough to be rather proud of."[2] On July 10,
at Laurel Hill, he and a handful of other Union recruits
haphazardly attacked a Confederate breastworks. As the
startled youths faced a hail of Southern bullets, Bierce
scooped up a fatally wounded comrade, Corporal Dyson
Boothroyd, and scurried to cover more than a hundred
yards away.[3]

The Ninth Indiana, as part of a brigade commanded by
Brigadier General William Rosecrans, also participated in
Union victories at Rich Mountain and Carrick's Ford, July
11-13. Late that month the regiment returned to Indian-

apolis and was discharged, having completed its short tour of duty. When the unit was reorganized for three years, Bierce reenlisted at La Porte, Indiana, on August 14, 1861, as a sergeant, rising to sergeant-major shortly after the regiment was mustered in on September 5. It returned to the West Virginia Cheat Mountains for the winter, participating in a skirmish at Greenbrier (October 3) and an attack on Camp Allegheny at Buffalo Mountain (December 13). Both were Union defeats. But Bierce retained nostalgic memories of the entire area. After revisiting it in 1903, he wrote:

> The whole region is wild and grand, and if any one of the men who in his golden youth soldiered through its sleepy valleys and over its gracious mountains will revisit it in the hazy season when it is all aflame with the autumn foliage I promise him sentiments that he will willingly entertain and emotions that he will care to feel. Among them, I fear, will be a haunting envy of those of his comrades whose fall and burial in that enchanted land he once bewailed.[4]

III *Experienced Soldier*

Very shortly, however, Bierce was to see military action on a grand scale, with all its attendant confusions and alarms. In February, 1862, the Ninth Indiana was assigned to the Army of the Ohio and sent to Nashville to join Colonel William B. Hazen's Nineteenth Brigade of the Fourth Division for a month's intensive training. Henry Wager Halleck, Lincoln's General-in-Chief, planned to destroy the Confederate railroad center at Corinth, a swampy little town in northeastern Mississippi. To this end, Halleck ordered Buell's Army of the Ohio to join Grant's Army of the Tennessee at Shiloh, in southwestern Tennessee northeast of Corinth. Before Buell's arrival, however, the able Confederate commander at Corinth, General A. S. Johnston, launched a dawn offensive on April 6 against Grant's advance brigades at Pittsburg Landing, near Shiloh, two days' march east of Corinth on the west side of the Tennessee River.

Bierce later wrote that, because of their unsoldierly practice of sleeping undressed and of being unaware of the surprise attack because they had no pickets, "many of Grant's men when spitted on Confederate bayonets were as naked as civilians" ("The Mocking-Bird," *Works*, II, 219). Grant, convinced that the Confederates would not attack, was in Savannah, Tennessee, on the east side of the river several miles north of Shiloh. When he heard the battle begin, he hurried to join his men, who were cornered with only two small steamboats as an escape hatch. According to Bierce, Grant arrived at Pittsburg Landing only

> to find his camps in the hands of the enemy and the remnants of his beaten army cooped up with an impassable river at their backs for moral support. . . .
> Along the sheltered strip of beach between the river bank and the water was a confused mass of humanity—several thousands of men. They were mostly unarmed; many were wounded; some dead. All the camp-following tribes were there; all the cowards; a few officers. Not one of them knew where his regiment was, nor if he had a regiment. Many had not. These men were defeated, beaten, cowed. They were deaf to duty and dead to shame. . . .
> Whenever a steamboat would land, this abominable mob had to be kept off her with bayonets; when she pulled away, they sprang on her and were pushed by scores into the water, where they were suffered to drown one another in their own way.[5]

Meanwhile, "Bull" Nelson's Fourth Division, which was in the vanguard of Buell's army, had reached Savannah and rushed pell-mell to join Grant. Crossing the Tennessee River at Pittsburg Landing on April 6 and advancing all night through the rain, it participated in the second day of the battle, on April 7, 1862. Shiloh, with thousands of troops engaged, was the Ninth Indiana's first major encounter. But the regiment, with the highest casualties of any on the Union side, fought so heroically that it was commended by General Nelson. After Shiloh, the Ninth participated in Halleck's advance to Corinth. Bierce later wrote a bitter comment on both the Battle of Shiloh and this advance:

> The enemy, defeated in two days of battle at Pittsburgh Landing [Shiloh, where General Johnston had been killed], had sullenly retired to Corinth, whence he had come. For manifest incompetence Grant, whose beaten army had been saved from destruction and capture by Buell's soldierly activity and skill, had been relieved of his command, which nevertheless had not been given to Buell, but to Halleck, a man of unproved powers, a

theorist, sluggish, irresolute. Foot by foot his troops, always de-
ployed in line-of-battle to resist the enemy's bickering skirmishers, always entrenching against the columns that never
came, advanced across the thirty miles of forest and swamp toward an antagonist prepared to vanish at contact, like a ghost
at cock-crow. It was a campaign of "excursions and alarums,"
of reconnaissances and counter-marches, of cross-purposes and
countermanded orders. For weeks the solemn farce held attention, luring distinguished civilians from fields of political ambition to see what they safely could of the horrors of war.[6]

Finally, on May 28, Halleck's army reached Corinth. Then,
in July, Nelson's division was sent to Murfreesboro and
McMinnville after the raiding Confederate genius General
Nathan Bedford Forrest, who cut off his pursuers by destroying two railroad bridges south of Nashville. Hazen's
brigade repaired the railroad, and Hazen was in command
of the troops at Murfreesboro. In September, 1862, they
marched to Louisville—where Nelson was killed—and reformed.

Buell's Army of the Ohio fought an inconclusive battle
against General Bragg at Perryville in October; because of
its awkward performance there, it was reorganized as the
Army of the Cumberland to drive Bragg out of Tennessee.
Buell was called up for investigation and replaced as commander by General Rosecrans.

In November, 1862, Hazen became a Brigadier General,
commanding the Second Brigade (to which the Ninth Indiana Regiment was assigned) of the Second Division. On
December 1, Bierce was commissioned, on Hazen's recom-
mendation, a second lieutenant; despite some murmurings
from the soldiers in his company. Hazen, a West Pointer
and a Regular Army man, was a strict disciplinarian. Bierce
saw the necessity for, and adapted more readily to, military
discipline than most of his mates—a fact which probably accounts both for his promotion and for their umbrage at it.
Years later he wrote that the American volunteer "wants to
be a little general, deciding for himself, and is resentful of
the despotism necessary to his success and his welfare."[7]

A bitter battle was fought against Bragg at Stones River,
Tennessee, on December 31. Hazen's brigade, strongly entrenched in a four-acre oak grove called the Round Forest,
or "Hell's Half Acre," bore the brunt of Bragg's attack; and

the Ninth Indiana was in the very thick of the fighting.
Bierce later used this battle as the background for "A Resumed Identity," a story whose protagonist had been a lieutenant on General Hazen's staff and was wounded. In the
actual battle, Bierce rescued the fallen Major Braden, commander of the Ninth Indiana; then, on Hazen's recommen-
dation, Bierce was promoted to first lieutenant.

In January, 1863, Rosecrans' Army of the Cumberland
was divided into three corps with a fourth corps in reserve:
the Army of Kentucky, under Major General Gordon
Granger. In March, 1863, Hazen transferred Bierce to brigade headquarters for a month as provost marshal, and on
April 4 made him acting topographical engineer. He continued to serve as acting topographical officer through the
rest of the war; his military notebook has maps of Tennessee, Georgia, and Alabama. The responsibilities of this staff
assignment he later used to characterize the narrator of his
story "George Thurston" (*Works*, II, 209-10):

> Whether in camp or on the march, in barracks, in tents, or *en
> bivouac*, my duties as topographical engineer kept me working
> like a beaver—all day in the saddle and half the night at my
> drawing-table, platting my surveys. It was hazardous work; the
> nearer to the enemy's lines I could penetrate, the more valuable
> were my field notes and the resulting maps. It was a business in
> which the lives of men counted as nothing against the chance
> of defining a road or sketching a bridge. Whole squadrons of
> cavalry escort had sometimes to be sent thundering against a
> powerful infantry outpost in order that the brief time between
> the charge and the inevitable retreat might be utilized in sound-
> ing a ford or determining the point of intersection of two
> roads.

But Bierce's task was humanized by his friendship with
another member of Hazen's staff—Sherburne Blake Eaton, a
captain in the 124th Ohio Infantry Regiment. Bierce was
professionally associated with Eaton, a Yale graduate
slightly older than he, at two subsequent periods in their
careers. Moreover, he admired and liked the stern Hazen, a
feeling which was reciprocated. Years later they praised
each other in print, Hazen referring to Bierce as "a brave
and gallant fellow," while Bierce returned the compliment
by calling Hazen an "excellent soldier and born fighter."[8]

The young staff officer was particularly impressed by Hazen's coolness in battle, contrasting it with the flamboyance of Rosecrans: "I once saw the late Gen. Hazen ride leisurely into a hot action without a weapon of any kind, not even a spur. He carried a hazel switch. Gen. Rosecrans, on the contrary, was addicted to the vice of galloping wildly along in rear of the front line of his army, making a spectacular extravaganza of himself, with his entire glittering retinue thundering at his heels."[9]

Bierce's next important engagement, at Chickamauga on September 19 and 20, 1863, involved so much shifting of men and such faulty intelligence that both Rosecrans and Bragg had only the scantiest information about troop deployment. When the right Federal wing collapsed, Rosecrans, thinking his entire army was being destroyed, fled to Chattanooga. Major General George Henry Thomas, however, commanding the left wing, stood firm, supported by Granger in direct violation òf orders; and the Union army was thus saved from complete rout. The Ninth Indiana fought so valiantly that it was commended by Hazen. This bloody battle not only gave Bierce an opportunity to visit his brother Albert, who was in the Eighteenth Ohio Field Artillery under Granger; it also furnished the background for the magnificent story "Chickamauga."[10]

As a result of his defection, Rosecrans was relieved of his command, and the Army of the Cumberland was turned over to Thomas. Its Fourth Corps sustained the highest battle losses of any in the Western theater of operations. Hazen was in charge of the Second Brigade of its Third Division, commanded by Brigadier General Thomas John Wood, while the Ninth Indiana was part of the First Division.

After the battle of Chickamauga, Bragg pursued the Federal army to Chattanooga. Generals Thomas, Howard, and Hooker, leading the Union troops there, were joined by reinforcements under General Burnside, in east Tennessee; and General Sherman, who was hastening to join them. This greatly augmented army was placed under the overall charge of General Grant, who arrived in Chattanooga to take command.

On November 24-25 occurred the Union victories of Lookout Mountain and Missionary Ridge. In the latter, the

Ninth Indiana spearheaded an assault against Bragg's left
flank, while Wood's Division was one of four in the front
line of battle facing the Confederates and the first to storm
the summit of the ridge against an entrenched enemy.
Grant's orders were that the troops should halt and reform
after an initial assault; but, discovering that such tactics
would expose them to murderous fire, the junior officers
and men charged immediately up the hill on their own ini-
tiative. In this battle, Bierce surveyed the field and, as a
staff officer, carried the order to attack to Colonel James
C. Foy, 23rd Kentuckians, in Wood's Division. "The loss of
Chattanooga [in which Grant proved his superb generalship
and Bragg narrowly missed capture] was a severe blow to
the dying Confederate cause. A vital line of lateral com-
munications was lost, and the stage was set for Sherman's
move to split the Confederacy further by his Atlanta campaign and march to the sea."[11]

IV *Disillusioned Officer*

On December 12, 1863, the Ninth Indiana's service expired; but the entire regiment reenlisted and was given a
long furlough. Bierce returned to Warsaw, where he became
engaged to Tima Wright, though he grew almost equally
fond of her sister Clara. His furlough ended in February,
1864, and for the third time he left home with the Ninth
Indiana. In May, he was detached from his regiment to remain on the staff of Hazen's brigade of the Third Division
of the Fourth Corps, which was now commanded by Major
General O. O. Howard. This was a part of the 98,000-man
army Sherman was preparing for his campaign against Atlanta and to confront the Confederate Generals Joseph
Eggleston Johnston and John B. Hood. A series of skirmishes in Georgia at Rocky Face Ridge, Dalton, Resaca,
and New Hope Church followed.

Then, on May 27, 1864, in the minor battle of Pickett
Mill, Georgia, Generals Wood and Howard, criminally mis-
guided, ordered Hazen's single brigade on a suicidal mission
against two divisions of General Johnston's army. Hazen's
already decimated brigade was cut to pieces.[12] And on
June 8 the disillusioned young Bierce, who had not heard
from his fiancée for nearly a month, wrote her sister a

pathetic letter from Ackworth, Georgia, saying "I am getting very tired of my present life and weary of the profession of arms. . . . Since leaving Cleveland Tenn. my brigade has lost nearly one third its numbers killed and wounded. . . . My turn will come in time. . . . It is raining very hard and I am very lonely."[13]

The letter was prophetic. On June 10, 1864, three weeks' fighting began at Kenesaw Mountain, Georgia, for which Bierce drew maps, and which he later used as background for "One of the Missing" (*Works*, II, 71-92). On June 23 he was dangerously wounded in the head and carried to his brother's tent. Albert, now in the Seventh Battery of the Indiana Light Artillery, saved his life by giving him first aid. Ambrose was hospitalized in Chattanooga; and, when he was discharged in July, he was sent home on convalescent leave. There he whiled away the time by reading James Russell Lowell's "The Washers of the Shroud" in *The Atlantic*. More importantly, he and Tima broke their engagement for reasons which can only be conjectured.

In late September, 1864, Bierce rejoined the Fourth Army Corps. Hazen was transferred, but Bierce continued as acting topographical engineer on the staff of Hazen's successor, Colonel P. Sidney Post, heading the Second Brigade of the Third Division, who probably requested Bierce's assignment. In October, 1864, Bierce designed and superintended the construction of an extensive fortification at Pulaski, Tennessee, as part of Sherman's March to the Sea.

Meanwhile, the Fourth Corps joined Major General John McAllister Schofield's Twenty-third Corps; and early in November these troops set off for Nashville to assist General Thomas against Hood, who was trying to check Sherman's advance. After a forced march to Franklin, Schofield led the Union troops to a Federal victory there on November 30, which Bierce later wrote up in "What Occurred at Franklin" (*Works*, I, 315-27). Schofield then withdrew to a strong position at Nashville, where Bierce was transferred—still as topographical officer—to the headquarters of the Third Division, commanded by Brigadier General Samuel Beatty of Ohio. Bierce's slightly fictionalized account of this period follows:

> The enemy had driven us up out of northern Georgia and Alabama. At Nashville we had turned at bay and fortified, while old Pap Thomas, our commander, hurried down reinforcements and supplies from Louisville. Meantime Hood, the Confederate commander, had partly invested us and lay close enough to have tossed shells into the heart of the town. As a rule he abstained—he was afraid of killing the families of his own soldiers, I suppose, a great many of whom had lived there. . . .
>
> . . . On that bleak December morning a few days later, when from an hour before dawn until ten o'clock we sat on horseback on those icy hills, . . . there were eight of us. At the close of the fighting there were three.[14]

In the battle of Nashville on December 15-16, 1864, Thomas' army defeated Hood's Confederates through brilliant strategy and tactics. The only significant setback the Federal troops incurred was in a charge on Overton Hill, in which Colonel Post was killed while leading the Second Brigade of Beatty's Division. The greatest Union regimental loss was suffered by the 13th United States Colored Infantry. Later Bierce wrote an interesting account of this aspect of the battle. He had at one time, he said, asked for assignment as field officer of Negro troops. On second thoughts, however, he had canceled the request.

> But at the battle of Nashville it was borne in upon me that I had made a fool of myself. During the two days of that memorable engagement the only reverse sustained by our arms was in an assault upon Overton Hill, a fortified salient of the Confederate line, on the second day. The troops repulsed were a brigade of Beatty's division and a colored brigade of raw troops which had been brought up from a camp of instruction at Chattanooga. I was serving on Gen. Beatty's staff, but was not doing duty that day, being disabled by a wound—just sitting in the saddle and looking on. Seeing the darkies going in on our left I was naturally interested and observed them closely. Better fighting was never done. The front of the enemy's earthworks was protected by an intricate abatis of felled trees denuded of their foliage and twigs. Through this obstacle a cat would have made slow progress; its passage by troops under fire was hopeless from the first—even the inexperienced black chaps must have known that. They did not hesitate a moment: their long lines swept into that fatal obstruction in perfect order and remained there as long as those of the white veterans on their right. And

as many of them in proportion remained until borne away and buried after the action. It was as pretty an example of courage and discipline as one could wish to see.[15]

Following this battle, the Union troops went into winter quarters in Huntsville, northern Alabama. There, on January 10, 1865, Bierce tendered his resignation on grounds of physical disability. He was not, however, mustered out immediately; for he was to accompany Sherman, who after his March to the Sea had been ordered to proceed north from Savannah to Goldsboro, North Carolina. On this march, which covered 425 miles in fifty days, rather than the more famous march through Georgia, Sherman's military reputation rests. Primarily a grueling and exhausting battle against the elements rather than enemy forces, its strategic importance was enormous.

Bierce's participation in this Carolinas Campaign is detailed in his Civil War notebook. He records that on January 21 he was in Beaufort, South Carolina, and entries from then until March 24 show that the members of his unit were almost constantly on the move: skirmishing; repairing and constructing roads and bridges; destroying railroads and munitions dumps; crossing creeks, rivers, and swamps; camping in fields and deserted farm houses. On February 17, they entered Columbia, South Carolina, where they stayed three nights. And on February 24, they captured a Confederate officer, Captain Devoux. On March 12, they reached Fayetteville, North Carolina; on March 24, Goldsboro. By the latter date they had marched 461½ miles; corduroyed 17,417 yards of road; cut 223 miles of side roads for troops; and constructed 4,850 feet of bridge. On April 26, 1865, the Confederate General Johnston surrendered to Sherman (Lee had surrendered to Grant on April 9), and the long and bloody strife was over.

Contrary to previously published statements, Bierce was not discharged on January 16, 1865; his actual release probably did not come until late March or April. Consequently, he served from the beginning to the end of our most tragic conflict; its impress haunted him for the rest of his life.

CHAPTER 2

Quest for Identity

FOR the next seven years Bierce was occupied in the effort to find out who and what he was. The cessation of war meant the beginning of major readjustments in his life; and, like other young veterans before and after him, he embarked on a series of abortive careers in a restless effort to establish himself.

I Treasury Agent

From April until autumn, 1865, he worked in Alabama commandeering Confederate cotton for the United States Treasury Department. He assisted his friend and former fellow officer on Hazen's staff, Sherburne Eaton, who was in charge of the First Agency in Alabama, with headquarters in New Orleans. In this chaotic period, bribery, graft, and corruption were rampant, foreshadowing the scandals of the carpetbaggers. Bierce, always a man of sterling honesty, was disgusted by this depravity and remained untainted by it. He was also proof against the hostility between Federal agents and the Alabamans who had but recently been their enemies; Bierce had, indeed, two cronies who were ex-Confederate officers.[1] Ominously, however, he began suffering the asthma attacks which were to plague him all the rest of his life.

In April, Bierce had established his headquarters in Selma, central Alabama, formerly an important military center which had just been gutted by Union cavalry. The town was a shambles, noisome with the stench of death; and its facilities for law and order were completely disrupted. Bierce made maps and surveys, occasionally reporting to Eaton at New Orleans. The controversial regime of Major General Ben Butler had been in force there in 1862; and Butler's notorious "Woman Order," which authorized his officers and soldiers to treat the women of New Orleans as prostitutes, had provoked Lord Palmerston's declaration to the British House of Commons that "an Englishman must blush to think that such an act has been committed by one belonging to the Anglo-Saxon race."[2] Such embarrassing policies as these had, however, resulted in Butler's replacement; and the full havoc of Reconstruction had not yet struck the city, which captivated Bierce with its charm.

II *Tourist*

In September, while on a holiday in New Orleans, Bierce sailed on the steamer *Sacramento* for Colón (then called Aspinwall), Panama. He was immediately impressed with the "free and easy impudence of the native black boys" who sought to carry his luggage. He was also taken with the tropical vegetation—cane, four kinds of palms, roses, lemons and oranges, and various unidentified plants and trees. He drew diagrams of some of these in an account of his trip which is still extant; he printed his record in pencil, with execrable spelling and indifferent punctuation, but in a small, very neat hand. This notebook[3] bears testimony to the keenness of his observation. He noted "a throng of natives, mostly women, pedling fruits and confectionary." The cleanliness of their dresses formed a pleasing contrast to the universal filth he noticed everywhere.

Aspinwall is built on a coral reaf.... The main part of the town is built of slovenly wooden howses back of these are Palm hutts. Some pleasent houses there are on the esplanade.... The throngs of great black buzzards sitting on every roof and tree, and hopping fearlessly about in the offall strewn streets was in keeping with the general appearance. The people cut beaf into long stripes and hang it on racks in the sun to dry. One of these racks I noticed the buzzards were watching. suddenly a dairing old fellow hopped towards it; flapping up amongst the long tempting slices commenced a ravenous attack, at this a half nude old woman rushed out upon him with cries and after repeatedly walloping him over the head with a towl succeeded in driving him off.

After lunch, Bierce took a train ride through the tropical malarial swamps surrounding Aspinwall to Panama, "a quaint old town almost crowded into the sea By the Mountains." Here he boarded the steamer again: "The Bay of Panama is full of little Islands—is very Shole so that Steamers have to lie out 3 miles. Passengers are taken out in a kind of steam-ferry. The bay is full of larg fish, sharks &c. that, dashing about make a beautiful display of its phosphorescence."

On September 17, Bierce arrived at Acapulco, and then returned to New Orleans. There he found a letter awaiting him from General Hazen, whom the War Department had ordered to make a mapping and surveying expedition westward through the Indian country; he was to inspect military posts and fortresses from Omaha to San Francisco. Hazen, who offered Bierce a post as engineering attaché on this tour, recommended that he apply for a captaincy in the Regular Army. Because the prospect of adventure appealed to Bierce, and the rank satisfied him, he accepted Hazen's offer.

III *The Overland Trail*

Prior to leaving, he returned to his parents' farm in Indiana for a visit, staying until early summer. He then joined Hazen's group, which also included a cook, a teamster, and a small cavalry detachment. Although his commission had not yet arrived, Bierce was assigned to make surveys and sketches on the Western expedition. The party set out from Omaha in July, 1866, following the Platte River to Fort Kearney. The country, though pleasant and productive, was dotted with rude graves and piles of bleached bones. But travel for the first two hundred miles, in the valley of the Platte, was easy; and Bierce's asthma began to clear up under the healthy outdoor regimen.

In the meantime, a telegram had reached Elkhart with the news of his commission as a second lieutenant. But "Captain" Bierce, unaware of his diminished rank, was heading northwest over a road that had become a mere buffalo trail toward Fort Smith, in the foothills of the Big

Horn Mountains. There the expedition was ordered, with typical army logic, to return to Washington via Salt Lake City, San Francisco, and Panama. Hazen disobeyed and continued northwest up the Missouri River in the territory of Montana to inspect Fort Benton. This part of the trip was strenuous: food was scarce, water acrid with alkali, mountains had to be climbed and rivers swum, and Indian attack (never, however, realized) was a constant menace. The bedraggled party arrived at Fort Benton hungry and parched with thirst, then traveled south along the Missouri River and the Sun to the Rockies and the Yellowstone Valley, arriving in late September at the boom mining towns of Helena and Virginia City, Montana.

Bierce's duties were not heavy; for him, the expedition was like a camping trip.[4] At the military posts the group was welcomed with food, drink, and such merrymaking as could be supplied while Hazen conducted his painstaking inspections. Bierce, who was much taken with the grandeur of the magnificent scenery, sketched pictures and copied Indian inscriptions in addition to drawing his maps. This material is preserved in a notebook he kept, which is inscribed: "A. G. Bierce, Route Maps of a Journey from Fort Laramie—Dakota Terr. to Fort Benton—Montana Territory 1866." These data, with some additions showing the Black Hills, were published in San Francisco more than ten years later.

The party next traveled across southeastern Idaho to Salt Lake City, where they stayed about ten days while Hazen interviewed Brigham Young. Bierce, who was much impressed by the Mormons, was later to excoriate their persecutors. From Salt Lake City, the expedition went, in late October, across Nevada and the Sierras. It followed the new roadbed of the Central Pacific to Sacramento in November, then proceeded to San Francisco.

All this time Bierce's commission as a second lieutenant had been trying to catch up with him. A telegram from Washington finally reached him in San Francisco on April 3, 1867. Incensed at not receiving the captaincy he had expected, he wired back on April 4: "I respectfully decline the appointment."[5] He thereupon resigned from Hazen's expedition in disgust, deciding to stay in California. On May 9, however, he acknowledged the receipt of a commis-

sion as brevet major of volunteers,[6] a purely honorary title
awarded for distinguished military service. On June 22,
1867, when a general order was issued breveting thousands
of Union officers to the next higher rank, Bierce was listed
among this group as a major. If his honorary promotion
had gone through routine channels, he would, of course,
have been made a captain. One wonders, accordingly,
whether General Hazen, indignant at the shabby treatment
given his protégé, may not have pulled strings to get him
the higher rank based on the commission he had been
promised for the Western expedition, especially since notification of his majority reached him a month and a half
before the date of the general order.

But for the immediate future, faced with the problem of
earning a livelihood, Bierce applied at the United States
Sub-Treasury in San Francisco (connected with the Mint
but a separate institution) for a government job. He was
appointed a night watchman at an annual salary of $1,500;
later he advanced to memorandum clerk. Bierce impressed
his early San Francisco associates with his military carriage,
dignity, geniality, and charm—but, above all, by his outspoken irreverence; for he lost no opportunity to lacerate
their pious sensibilities with gibes at subjects they held
sacred.

IV *To Train a Writer*

During this period, Bierce began seriously the arduous
task of turning himself into a writer. When one remembers
the notebook passage describing his trip to Panama, sprinkled with misspelled words, grammatical errors, and mistakes in punctuation, one realizes the magnitude of his
chore. He devoted himself to a heavy reading schedule,
having frequent recourse to *Webster's Unabridged Dictionary*. When questioned, he revealed the reason for his labo-
rious program of self-education: "It is my ambition to
write books," he announced, "and to do this well you must
be acquainted with the language and be a master at the use
of words."[7]

A comparison of his 1865 journal with his mature works
is a startling revelation of how thoroughly he implemented,
in his own training, the theories he eventually propounded.
"How to use a language," he wrote many years later, "must

be acquired by special and systematic effort."[8] Skill in expression, though difficult to achieve, was a technical accomplishment which could be attained partly, at least, through devoted study.

Bierce's duties in the Sub-Treasury sat lightly on his shoulders, and he devoted all his spare time to writing atheistic tracts and to drawing political lampoons. When the cartoons were circulated without his permission, however, he stopped doing them and concentrated on writing. At first his style was hyperbolic, ironic bombast, in the tradition of frontier humor exemplified by Dan De Quille and the early Mark Twain. But Bierce was soon fortunate enough to acquire as friend and tutor a polished and scholarly Englishman, James Watkins, who assigned him a course of reading which included Shakespeare, Swift, Voltaire, La Rochefoucauld, Balzac, and Thackeray.

Watkins, himself master of a flexible and elegant style, had been a journalist in London and New York; and he was at this time managing editor of *The San Francisco News Letter and California Advertiser*, owned by another Englishman, Frederick A. Marriott. This publication was the company organ of the Aerial Steam Navigation Company, interested in promoting air flight with a balloon called the "Avitor" that Bierce occasionally ascended in.

His first known published works were two derivative and undistinguished poems, "Basilica" and "A Mystery," which appeared in the *Californian* on September 21 and November 18, 1867, respectively. But he wrote later: "When I was in my twenties, I concluded one day that I was not a poet. It was the bitterest moment of my life."[9] Although he continued to write verse, he shifted his attention to prose, publishing an essay on "Female Suffrage" in a December issue of the *Californian* and, in July and September, 1868, essays in *The Golden Era*. Both these periodicals were edited by James F. Bowman, who became one of his close friends.

Bierce was also writing sketches for the *News Letter*, and he probably joined its staff in the late summer of 1868. In December, when Watkins resigned, he induced Marriott to give his post to Bierce, who thereupon surrendered his job in the Sub-Treasury and, on December 12, 1868, became editor of the *News Letter*. At the same time, he took over

a column which had been a regular feature of the paper,
"The Town Crier"; in Bierce's hands, its ferocious, Rabelai-
sian wit and stinging satire became famous; for his quips
were widely quoted and admired in New York and even in
London. In return, he published a poem by Algernon
Charles Swinburne in the *News Letter* on December 25,
1869.

Bierce had also met Bret Harte, who was secretary of the
Mint and who became editor of *The Overland Monthly*.
Bierce submitted to him, probably in December, 1870, a
series of papers which he thought might be "suitable for a
regular department." These were not hastily tossed off journalism; he had spent much time and effort on them, re-
vising and polishing and "trying to avoid, on the one hand,
the Scylla of Bret-Hartism and on the other, the Charybdis
of the Town Crier." He signed the papers "Ursus," leaving
their christening up to Harte.[10] These essays began appearing as the "Grizzly Papers" in the January, 1871, issue of
The Overland Monthly. When Harte resigned in a huff with
the owner, John H. Carmany, and left for the East, Bierce
continued to write for it. But his relations with Carmany
were not exactly amicable. Bierce began referring to the
magazine as the "Warmed-overland Monthly"; he objected to
the prices he was paid; and he complained because the new
editor, William C. Bartlett, was making excessive alterations
in his copy—something Harte had never done. Taking a high-
handed tone, Bierce threatened to quit writing for the journal
unless his material was printed as it was submitted.

Five "Grizzly Papers" appeared: in January, February,
March, April, and June of 1871. They contain some of
Bierce's best and most distinctive early work. Allusions to
John Stuart Mill, Henry Buckle, Viscount Bolingbroke,
Samuel Taylor Coleridge, Francis Bacon, John Ruskin,
"Novalis," Empedocles, Voltaire, and Plato give evidence of
the wide range of his reading. Characteristic Biercean ideas
and themes, sprinkled with Latin tags, begin to appear. On
the subject of self-reliance, he wrote that "If a man have a
broad foot, a stanch leg, a strong spine, and a talent for
equilibrium, there is no good reason why he should not
stand alone . . . . A mind that is right side up does not need
to lean upon others: it is sufficient unto itself. The curse of
our civilization is that the 'association' is become the unit,

and the individual is merged in the mass."[11] He attacked conformity to public opinion, which he thought fickle and mediocre. Differences of nationality, intelligence, profession or vocation, and breeding create individual variations; and civilization has advanced because of the minority which had the courage not to kowtow to the powerful majority.

Bierce also outlined his views on the tentativeness of human knowledge. One should reserve judgment on problems which cannot be solved by reason, he believed, rather than leap blindly into an uncritical acceptance of dogma by faith. In this connection, he was not writing particularly about theological matters but about social, moral, ethical, political, and even scientific ones. "A natural law is not mandatory: it can be neither obeyed nor disobeyed. We will say that the law of gravitation is this: All bodies tend to approach one another. That is not saying that they must, but that they do. A natural law is but a statement—a record of observed facts."[12]

He also propounded some interesting theories on esthetics, attacking, for example, the heresy of the didactic. In literature, as in art, he believed, "the question of morality is a question of the second rank . . . . The test of excellence [in a literary work] is the pleasure it carries to the more cultivated and discerning of the class to which it is addressed." And he was struck with the restraint and control exercised by good poetry: "It is more than a little singular that the passions, which burn with a lawless flame, and the imagination, which flies with a free wing, should find their largest liberty in confinement; in other words, that these unruly qualities should be best expressed in the measure and exact diction of verse . . . . Why our most spontaneous and tumultuous feelings go voluntarily into harness, is a very . . . difficult question."[13]

In June, Bierce wrote Bartlett that his inspiration for the "Grizzly Papers" had waned and that he did not want to continue the series with inferior material since "a palpable falling off" would be injudicious. He announced, however, that he was working on a story which would be even better than the "Grizzlies."[14] This story, Bierce's first to be published, appeared under the title "The Haunted Valley" in the July, 1871, issue of *The Overland Monthly*; it was later reprinted in *Can Such Things Be?*

V *Marriage*

Ambrose's asthma had recurred soon after his arrival in San Francisco. To escape its ravages, he moved across the bay north of the Golden Gate to the pretty little summer
– resort of San Rafael. His circle of friends was widening to include most of the local literati. In addition to Watkins, Bowman, and Harte, these included Charles Warren Stoddard, who, like Bierce, was a contributor to the *Alta California*; Ina Coolbrith; Edward Rowland Sill; and Prentice Mulford. In San Rafael Bierce met, probably early in 1870, an attractive young woman named Mary Ellen ("Mollie") Day whom he began squiring around. Born in Galena, Illinois, she was the only daughter in a New York State Dutch family. Her father, Holland Hines Day, who had come to California in the wake of the "49-ers," was prominent in mining and politics in Nevada and Utah.

While Captain Day was off to the mines, his wife lived in a handsome San Francisco house with her son James and her daughter, a lively, witty girl who played the piano and sang. Mollie saw much of Bierce during the summer of 1871; they made a twosome in a circle of friends, including Stoddard and Ina Coolbrith, and were soon engaged. In February, 1870, Bierce had publicly twitted Mark Twain for his marriage to a rich woman; but on December 25, 1871, he followed suit. He and Mollie were married by a Unitarian minister in the Days' house in a simple ceremony with only friends present.

The young couple settled down in San Rafael and Ambrose became a charter member of the famous Bohemian Club, founded by his friend Jimmy Bowman. But Joaquin Miller had recently returned from a triumphal sojourn in England and arranged to meet Bierce. Miller had had a tremendous success with the Rossetti brothers and Swinburne, who had praised his work to Matthew Arnold, and he probably told glowing tales about the country which had received him so royally. Playing the role of the wild and woolly Westerner, he had attended gatherings at Ford Madox Brown's wearing a bright red cowboy shirt and muddy riding boots. Englishmen were apparently avid for such rustic phenomena, for Swinburne wrote Frederick Locker on May 17, 1871: "I always thought the Far West of America would produce better and more national poets than the Boston school; and this Californian sample is racy of new soil and strong sunlight."[15]

Bierce, who had himself been getting letters from London praising his Town Crier column, decided to emigrate. On March 9, 1872, he resigned from the *News Letter*; and, financed by Captain Day and armed by Frederick Marriott with letters of introduction to London journalists, he left with Mollie for England.

CHAPTER 3

Transatlantic Sojourn

I *Anglophile*

IN later years Ambrose Bierce regarded his stay in England
from 1872 to 1875 as "the happiest and most prosperous
period of his life."[1] The newlyweds found London a delightful place, overrun by Americans whom they were constantly
meeting at such standard tourist attractions as Trafalgar
Square, St. Paul's, Westminster Abbey, the theaters, and the
Tower of London. Bierce described with relish a boat race on
the Thames in which an American team was defeated by the
British, the horse races at Derby and Ascot, a concert, and his
visits with other journalists. Moreover, he found London "the
cleanest of cities" and British officials much more honest
than their American counterparts. He also acquired a lasting
impression of "the Englishman" as "a warm-hearted chap—a
sentimentalist a little ashamed of sentiment."[2] He was
charmed, too, with the English railway, which he deemed
greatly superior to its American analogue. As if all this were
not enough, he found it cheaper to live in England "than to
loaf about the vicinity of New York." In short, he wrote,
"this is a better country, has nicer people, and is in every way
superior. You will infer from this that I like England. I do—
rather—ubette."

In his turn, Bierce made quite an impression. Now thirty,
he was a tall, handsome man, with gray eyes, a florid com-
plexion, and blond hair and mustache. His English friends
were struck with his lucid and logical mind and his sybaritic
tastes; for, however addicted he was to high thinking, the
debonair American was no devotee of plain living. He met his
share of notables: Robert Lincoln; Sir Henry Irving, the English actor; Sir Henry Lucy, who later had an Antarctic
mountain named after him; and Swinburne, whom Bierce

characterized as a weak-faced, shifty-eyed little marionette who jerked about as if he were manipulated by strings. According to Bierce, "Mr. Swinburne has brains, or he could not write the verse he does; he is insane, or he would not." Bierce's love of and admiration for England lasted all his life. After his return to America he wrote:

> The glories of England are our glories. She can achieve nothing that our fathers did not help to make possible to her . . . . The American eulogist of civilization who is not proud of his heritage in England's glory is unworthy to enjoy his lesser heritage in the lesser glory of his own country.
>
> The English are undoubtedly our intellectual superiors; and as the virtues are solely the product of intelligence and cultivation —a rogue being only a dunce considered from another point of view—they are our moral superiors likewise.[3]

Yet Bierce, a sensitive and discerning man, saw clearly that all was not sweetness and light on the English scene. In particular, he was horrified at the brutalized and half-starved condition of the British agricultural workers, whose plight moved him to sharp compassion and to a stinging condemnation of the society that fostered such misery. Shortly after his arrival he wrote: "I know of no more wretched class than the English farm laborers; and their existence in their present degraded state would be a lasting reproach to the Government, if only that had ever aided and abetted their existence in any state. When a man can ride all day in a direct line across his estates, and in so doing pass a thousand doors behind which Want crouches with hollow eyes, there is something radically wrong in the system under which that man lives."

For the most part, however, his judgment of England remained favorable: "I do not hold that the political and social system that creates an aristocracy of leisure is the best possible kind of human organization; I perceive its disadvantages clearly enough. But I do hold that a system under which most important public trusts, political and professional, civil and military, ecclesiastical and secular, are held by educated men—that is, men of trained faculties and disciplined judgment—is not an altogether faulty system."[4]

II *Man of Letters*

Bierce very quickly became active on the London journalistic and publishing fronts. Almost immediately he began writing for *Fun*, a humorous weekly edited by Tom Hood the Younger; preparing a column, "The Passing Showman," for *Figaro*, owned and edited by the vinegary American James Mortimer; and sending letters to the San Francisco *Alta California*, reporting on current events in England and the tourist sights he visited. He used the pen name "Dod Grile" in London, an anagram—as pointed out by Paul Fatout—for Douglas Jerrold ("Dg Ierold"), after whose melodrama, *Ambrose Gwinett; or, A Sea-side Story*, Bierce had been named.

Although Bierce saw such other California writers as Prentice Mulford, Mark Twain, Joaquin Miller, and Charles Warren Stoddard in England at one time or another during the period of his residence there, most of his social contacts were with newly acquired English friends. He spent many happy hours tippling with a Fleet Street gang, among whom George Augustus Sala and Tom Hood were the most notable topers. Hood remained Bierce's closest English friend until his death on November 20, 1874, when he was succeeded as editor of *Fun* by another of Bierce's friends, Henry Sampson. *Figaro*, which Bierce described as "a sharp little Frenchy publication," he remembered years later with sentimental fondness. Its editor, Mortimer, was "a Virginia fire-eater who was for some years dueling editor of a Parisian political sheet."

Bierce's first three books—*The Fiend's Delight, Nuggets and Dust*, and *Cobwebs from an Empty Skull*—were all published in London. The first two appeared in 1873 after a tangled history involving John Camden Hotten, the notorious London literary pirate and smut king.[5] Bierce began negotiations with him in July, 1872; and, after much bickering, *The Fiend's Delight* was published in the spring of 1873, shortly before Hotten's death on June 14. Bierce had concluded his arrangements with Hotten's manager, Andrew Chatto, while Hotten lay dying. Hotten's widow then sold his business to Chatto and Windus, who subsequently published Bierce's second book, *Nuggets and Dust*, which had been substantially ready for the press at the time Hotten suffered his fatal illness. During 1874 a third book of Bierce's, *Cobwebs from an Empty Skull*, was published by George Routledge and Sons. Like *The Fiend's Delight* and *Nuggets and Dust*, this work was a collection of his journalistic writings; it was reissued about 1884 by the *Fun* office with the truncated title *Cobwebs*.

A comparison of the books with their sources shows that Bierce was not merely copying his old material. Revision of some sort nearly always occurs, and occasionally the adaptation is extensive. A selection of his most interesting early work appears in these London volumes. "Current Journalings," third part of *The Fiend's Delight*, includes one amusingly wrong-headed piece of self-analysis (115-16): "We are tolerably phlegmatic and notoriously hard to provoke .... Slow to anger, quick to forgive, charitable in judgment and to mercy prone; with unbounded faith in the entire goodness of man and the complete holiness of woman; seeking ever for palliating circumstances in the conduct of the blackest criminal—we are at once a model of moderation and a pattern of forbearance."

"Laughorisms," from the same book, shows Bierce at his epigrammatic best:

> Those who are horrified at Mr. Darwin's theory, may comfort themselves with the assurance that, if we are descended from the ape, we have not descended so far as to preclude all hope of return.
> . . . .
> In the infancy of our language to be "foolish" signified to be affectionate; to be "fond" was to be silly. We have altered that now: to be "foolish" is to be silly, to be "fond" is to be affectionate. But that the change could ever have been made is significant.
> . . . .
> The noblest pursuit of Man is the pursuit of Woman.

"Notes Written with Invisible Ink by a Phantom American," the second section of *Nuggets and Dust*, includes appreciative little essays on aspects of England that had appealed to Bierce: "St. Paul's," "The Size of London," "Seeing a Journalist." "Stratford-on-Avon," one of the finest, was compared by his friend James T. Watkins, his predecessor as editor of the *News Letter*, to Washington Irving's appreciation of Shakespeare. These essays, which lack the tone of savage denunciation permeating much of Bierce's California writing, have a psychological interest—in addition to considerable literary merit—as indicating an alternative direction for his mental development had he settled permanently in an environment more congenial to him than the gilded corruption of late-nineteenth-century America.

"The Model Philosopher," also from *Nuggets and Dust*,
signed "Ursus" and adapted from the Grizzly Papers, reveals
Bierce's reading in philosophy (the tracks of Plato can be
clearly discerned, most notably in the little essay which treats
suicide as a Platonic myth [67-68]). This section is a series of
quasi-philosophical reflections on a multitude of topics, including the relativism of both physical perception and intellectual comprehension and the relation between Nature and
Art, a problem that continued to haunt Bierce as he developed his own esthetic theory.

Yet when these volumes appeared, Bierce professed contempt for them; and he continued to do so throughout his
life, dissuading publishers from reissuing them and diverting
attention to what he felt was his better work. Years afterward he referred to them as "youthful follies" consigned to
"benign oblivion"[6] which were "long (and deservedly) 'out
of print.' "[7] The basis for his continuing aversion probably
lies in their occasional lapses from style and even grammar—
and they do lack the clarity and precision of his prose at its
limpid best.

Yet these early publications are not so bad as Bierce
deemed them. Gladstone, twenty years after their original
appearance, started a Bierce boom in London by praising
their wit. A few items from them, such as the essay "Stratford-on-Avon" and some of the epigrams, have intrinsic
merit; several more, like the abortive tales "D.T." and "A
Working Girl's Story" in *Nuggets and Dust*, are of real importance to anyone who is interested in tracing their author's
artistic evolution. Bierce finally included parts of them, with
revisions, in his *Collected Works*. Since he called *The Fiend's
Delight* a "foolish book" at the very time he was plundering
it, it is instructive to note how much of it he himself actually
regarded as worthy of preservation. Three "Tall Talk" essays
from it were revised to reappear as TANGENTIAL VIEWS in
Volume IX: "A Call to Dinner" became "The Religion of the
Table" (*Works*, IX, 76-78); "Did We Eat One Another?" and
"Thanksgiving Day" were reprinted under the same titles (IX,
192-93 and 298-301). " 'Items' from the Press of Interior
California" were revised, and most of them were reprinted as
"Mortality in the Foot-Hills" (XII, 316-25). "Musings, Philo-
sophical and Theological," and "Laughorisms" from *The
Fiend's Delight* were combined with "The Model Philoso-

pher" from *Nuggets and Dust* and were then revised to form, with some additions, the EPIGRAMS (VIII, 343-81).

III *Peripatetic Expatriate*

Bierce's success in England was, therefore, almost immediate. But the damp London climate aggravated his chronic asthma, and toward the end of 1872 he and Mollie moved to Bristol, where their first child, a son, Day, was born in December. The new father was not eager to return to the capital because of the unfortunate effect the London fogs had on his lungs, and about the middle of February he moved with his family from Bristol to Bath. But in May, 1873, the Bierces returned to London, settling in Hampstead. That summer Mollie's mother, Mrs. Day, arrived for a visit; and in the autumn the whole family left for a month in Paris. When they returned to Hampstead, Bierce's mother-in-law took separate lodgings; but by the end of November Ambrose, Mollie, and the baby were back in Bath, where they were joined in January, 1874, by Mrs. Day. In the spring, the Bierces moved from Bath to Leamington, Warwickshire, where they lived for over a year. Mrs. Day was still with them, for Mollie was again pregnant. The Bierces' second son, Leigh, was born at Leamington on April 29, 1874. Shortly thereafter Mrs. Day, having seen her daughter through this accouchement, returned to San Francisco; and Mollie was left full responsibility for two infant sons and for a husband submerged by a flood of journalistic hack work.

Bierce continued to write for *Fun* and *Figaro*, and in addition had taken on a rather special job: the *Lantern*, a gorgeously polychromatic publication of which only two issues appeared, those of May 18 and July 15, 1874. These were subsidized by the widowed Empress Eugénie of France, then a wealthy exile in England, in order to copyright the title and forestall scurrilous attacks against her by the Communard Henri Rochefort, who was threatening to publish an English edition of his *La Lanterne*, which was notorious for its charges against the French imperial family. The *Lantern* was written entirely by Bierce, who had been recommended to the Empress by James Mortimer.

In the autumn of 1874, Tom Hood, who had been ailing for some time, became gravely ill and asked for Bierce, who was summoned by telegraph to London to see his dying friend. At their last interview Hood referred to a pact he and Bierce had made shortly before Bierce's move to Leamington, vowing that whichever of them died first should make an effort to communicate with the survivor. Hood died November 20, 1874; Bierce later claimed to have had two subsequent encounters with his "ghost," visitations which he explained on the grounds of synaesthesia: "the senses fool one another— . . . sight is translated into sound, or sudden and strong mental impressions are mistaken for tactual ones."[8]

Bierce maintained a desultory correspondence with his remaining English friends in London, and made several trips to the capital in the spring of 1875. One of these short trips was for the purpose of seeing his family off to America; for Mollie, who had decided to return home for a visit, left England with Day and Leigh on April 22. She was *enceinte* with their third child; but Bierce, unaware of his wife's condition, returned to Leamington, expecting to be rejoined by his family in the autumn. Lonely without his wife and babies, however, he moved to London in August.

But, learning of his wife's pregnancy, Bierce left England on the *Adriatic* in September, 1875, arriving in New York September 25,[9] and in San Francisco in early October, where he secured a job in the Branch Mint. His third child, a red-haired daughter, Helen, was born in San Francisco on October 30. Probably Bierce had wanted to settle in England, which he found very congenial and where—he told Gertrude Atherton years later—he would have stayed had it not been for his wife. But with four hostages to fortune, he was caught up in the exigencies of earning a living in America and of maintaining a family; the era of his expatriation was over, and he never saw Europe again.

CHAPTER 4

Hazards of Fortune

BIERCE'S unplanned return to America meant that he had, once again, to carve out a new career. Three possibilities were open—mining, journalism, and real estate. For over a decade his professional interests were divided among these fields, while he endeavored to establish himself as a solid citizen: a responsible husband and father of a growing family. After he came back to San Francisco, he joined Mollie and the boys at the Days' house. But he continued to suffer from asthma; and, after Helen's birth, he took his enlarged family to San Rafael. The change mitigated, though it did not dispel, his bronchial attacks; and by 1877 the Bierces were again living in San Francisco.

Ambrose had many friends in the city. Besides Judge John H. Boalt, the banker Charlie Kaufman, the photographer William Herman Rulofson, and the writer T. A. Harcourt, they included fellow members of the Bohemian Club: Jimmy Bowman, its founder, who wrote for the *Chronicle*; the Egyptologist Jeremiah Lynch; and the merchant E. L. G. Steele. Bierce was interested enough in the club's affairs to be elected secretary for 1876-77, but he resigned in 1878 because of its growing tendency to truckle to notabilities.

Early in 1876 Bierce learned from his brother Albert, who had married and settled in Oakland, that their father, Marcus Aurelius Bierce, was fatally ill. On February 13 Ambrose wrote his mother a heart-broken letter: "My poor Mother, I cannot write as I feel; you know what I would say; you know how dreadful is this affliction to me, who have not even the consolation of having been a good son to so good a father .... I can write no more for I am blind with tears."[1]

When Marcus died later that month in Elkhart, Indiana, at the age of seventy-seven, Bierce wrote his mother again on April 30:

I have delayed writing you for so long since receiving your sad account of the great grief which has fallen upon us all, only because I felt it too keenly for me to trust myself to write of it . . . .

I hope you will not for the present remain in Elkhart, but will go to your girls for at least a few months. But on this point Al has already written giving you his views and mine. He knows better than I, and in all things I defer to his superior judgment. Whatever he recommends I most cordially approve and will endeavor to assist in accomplishing.[2]

Two years later, in May, 1878, his mother also died.

After Bierce's return to California, his attention had begun to veer from writing to mining. Faced with the problem of earning a living, he had worked in the Assay Office of the Branch Mint for over a year. That it was a welcome meal ticket at the time is indicated by a verse he wrote after the definition of HOPE in *The Devil's Dictionary*:

> Delicious Hope! when naught to man is left—
> Of fortune destitute, of friends bereft;
> . . . . then thou,
> The star far-flaming on thine angel brow,
> Descendest, radiant, from the skies to hint
> The promise of a clerkship in the Mint.

Although he contributed an occasional Town Crier column and a poem, "Dies Irae," to the *News Letter*, he wrote Sampson in the spring of 1876 that he had eschewed journalism.

I *The* Argonaut

But he eventually resumed writing, indirectly because of the social and economic unrest which plagued California in the 1870s. The Central Pacific's Big Four—Mark Hopkins, Leland Stanford, Collis Huntington, and Charles Crocker— who were trying to force a bill through Congress giving them a railroad monopoly from Texas to California, had imported thousands of Chinese laborers to do menial work. When bank failures, depression, and unemployment struck, these Chinese workmen were ready scapegoats. And early in 1876 an Irish demagogue, Dennis Kearney, organized the Workingmen's Party of California—a rough and dangerous mob—on an anti-Chinese, anti-wealth platform.

A rich Republican and former United States District Attorney named Frank Pixley, who was a strong supporter of
Leland Stanford, finally decided to run Kearney out of
town. To this end he founded a magazine, the *Argonaut*,
hiring Fred Somers as co-editor and Bierce as associate
editor. The first issue appeared March 25, 1877. In addition
to French epigrams, the *Argonaut* published contributions
from Emma Frances Dawson; Annie Lake Townsend; Harcourt; Ina Coolbrith; Charles Warren Stoddard, who had
returned to America in the summer of 1877 after an extended sojourn on the Continent and in the Middle East;
William C. Morrow; and the poet Richard Realf.

But the outstanding feature of the magazine was a
column of wide-ranging comment by Bierce called "The
Prattler"—a title later changed to "Prattle"—which occasionally opposed editorial policy and in which a few definitions
that were to be the germ of *The Devil's Dictionary* appeared.[3] Bierce also continued the "Little Johnny" sketches
—a series of childishly misspelled commentaries on a variety
of subjects—that he had written for the London *Fun*.

In June, 1877, Bierce and Harcourt, financed by Rulofson, concocted an elaborate literary hoax, *The Dance of
Death*. Supposedly written by a "William Herman," it purported to be a vicious attack on the waltz; but it was so
suggestively written that it became a commercial success.
Bierce, who aided the imposture by stern strictures against
the book in "Prattle," was then answered by a Mrs. J.
Milton Bowers, who wrote *The Dance of Life*, which he
also denounced in a savage review. But he gave up his connection with the *Argonaut* in the spring of 1879, although
in 1880 Fred Somers, who had left it to edit *The Californian*, persuaded him to write a series of articles, "On With
the Dance!" for that magazine; in these Bierce berated not
only the prudish author of *The Dance of Death* but also
"Miss Nancy Howells" and "Miss Nancy James."

II *Miner*

In spite of these forays into writing, his really serious
efforts during this period were directed toward a detailed
investigation of various mining possibilities, particularly in
the Black Hills. As early as 1876 he had shown his interest
in this region by preparing a *Map of the Black Hills Region*,

*Showing the Gold Mining District and the Seat of the
Indian War. Drawn by A. G. Bierce from surveys ordered
by the War Department,* which was published by A. L.
Bancroft and Company of San Francisco in 1877. Although
Bierce's commission to do the work was undoubtedly based
on his Western tour with General Hazen, no indication
exists that he had, up to that time, ever visited the Black
Hills. Yet clearly his attention had been drawn there, and
in the spring of 1880 it focused on a particular spot.

Not far from the notorious Deadwood in the Dakota
Territory was the little mining town of Rockerville, which
had very rich gold deposits but no water for mining them.
If the nearby Spring Creek, however, could be dammed to
form a reservoir, and if the water could be transported over
a tortuous, seventeen-mile route, the problem would be
solved. The huge investment necessary for such a project
was acquired in New York on December 8, 1879, when the
Black Hills Placer Mining Company was incorporated with
capital stock of ten million dollars and a Wall Street office.
Intending not only to use the water itself for panning gold
on its own claims, but also to lease it to other miners who
had diggings there, the company planned to construct a
reservoir at Spring Creek and a seventeen-and-a-half-mile
box flume from the dam to Rockerville.

In New York, the company's president was General
Alexander Shaler, who had some military and social stand-
ing but not much reputation as a financier. Vice-president
John McGinnis, Jr., a broker, was an able businessman; and
Marcus Walker was secretary and treasurer. Sherburne Blake
Eaton, Bierce's old friend of Civil War and Reconstruction
days, was the legal adviser. On January 10, 1880, the com-
pany signed a contract with Captain Ichabod M. West, a
Rockerville adventurer and carpenter, to complete the dam
and flume by August 1, 1880, at a cost of $198,500.

But the infant company had misjudged its man and misplaced its trust. West reneged on his bills, though the well-
financed New York office kept him plentifully supplied
with funds. Unpaid laborers and subcontractors grew dis-
gruntled, local ill-feeling developed against the company,
and work fell far behind schedule. Back in New York,
McGinnis and Eaton persuaded Shaler and Walker, who

stoutly defended West, that West was at fault. And in the spring Bierce was engaged, on rather equivocal terms, as general agent of the Black Hills Placer Mining Company. It was understood that he was to take over West's job, and he departed for the Dakota Territory under that assumption, leaving Mollie and the children in California. By June 1, he was in Deadwood with Eddy S. Kaufman, a relative of Charlie's, who was investigating the possibility of establishing a branch of the family bank there. When this project collapsed, young Kaufman remained in Dakota as Bierce's secretary.

When Bierce arrived in Rockerville around the middle of June, only about a third of the work on the dam and the flume had been done. Belatedly, on June 18, the company's executive committee passed a resolution appointing Bierce its general agent in Dakota. But the resolution was not sent to Shaler, West, or Bierce, who were all in Rockerville; and almost a month passed before Bierce was officially notified of his appointment. Meanwhile, exasperated creditors were eager to be paid; the First National Bank of Deadwood held out $3,473.05 of company money against an overdraft of West's; and one of the stockholders sued him for embezzlement. West was arrested and tried in Deadwood, although the case was eventually dismissed; he then returned to Rockerville as the self-styled superintendent in opposition to Bierce. Shaler inexplicably supported West, and on July 1 treasurer Marcus Walker sent him a draft for $26,075, despite Bierce's formal appointment of June 18 as general agent. West by now had received $118,836 from Walker, but the job was less than half completed and the company owed thousands of dollars.

At this impasse, on July 7, the badgered executive committee in New York passed a second resolution that appointed Bierce general agent "to take charge of all the Company's matters in Dakota." But, instead of giving him full authority, the committee appointed a "Board of Advisement"—Shaler; Myron Willsie, a Black Hills civil engineer; and Bierce—which was to make all decisions by majority vote. So many conflicting orders were issued from the New York office that nobody knew who was boss. Bierce's situation in Rockerville was particularly difficult, in

spite of official recognition of his position on July 10,
when the June 18 resolution appointing him general agent
was transmitted to him.

On July 13 the company directors at long last fired West
and assumed responsibility for his debts. These proved to
be so large—reaching five figures—that eventually they
crushed the company. And Bierce made the mistake of
suing the First National Bank of Deadwood in his own
name for the $3,473.05 it held against West's overdraft,
thereby instituting interminable litigation—handled by
Daniel McLaughlin and William R. Steele, Deadwood attorneys—which dogged him for years. West and Shaler continued to hang meddlesomely around until midsummer,
when they went to New York.

Not only West's malpractices, however, but discord and
obstructionism in the Wall Street office hindered the development of the company's golden opportunities. One
group, headed by Shaler, continued to defend West, even
after his dismissal, and to attack Bierce; the other faction,
led by McGinnis and Eaton, supported the general agent.
The directors, who had rained money on the dishonest and
inefficient West, were growing reluctant to send good dollars after bad just at the time Bierce was assuming responsibility.

Twice Bierce asked McGinnis to hire a detective to track
down West's fraud, but his immediate problem was lack of
funds. He instituted stringent economies, beginning with
himself. He did the janitorial work in his office and had
only a skeleton staff; moreover, he paid Eddy Kaufman—
secretary, bookkeeper, and general handyman—from his
own funds. He retrenched further by stalling creditors, de-
laying lawsuits, and cutting down the labor force. He did,
however, hire a gunman, Boone May, to fight off stage-
coach bandits and to protect company money; Bierce
carried him on the payroll as "Boone May, murderer."[4]
Yet in spite of these drastic measures, on August 1 the
flume was nowhere near finished; and the company was
running out of funds.

Nevertheless, Bierce, who had faith in the project,
pleaded desperately for more money to continue the work
and begged Eaton to visit Rockerville. But Marcus Walker,
who finally came, arrived prepared to prove Bierce a crook.

He and his cohorts criticized the general agent so arrogantly that, after several days of heroic self-control, Bierce lost his temper. Although the inquisitors henceforth treated him more politely and found his books in good order, Walker continued to distrust him; and, just as an uneasy truce was being negotiated, the secretary-treasurer dashed back to Wall Street. There he presented a trumped-up list of accusations against Bierce and his backers. The hearing that Bierce demanded was not granted, and Walker filed formal charges against him.

In Rockerville, meanwhile, a second contingent of conspirators allied themselves with the Shaler-Walker bloc; for Walker had told the local miners that they could lease company water. This promise had caused them to turn against Bierce, whose plan had been to "dry them out" and then buy their mines so the company would have a monopoly. This ruthless but businesslike strategy was misunderstood and suspected in New York. Bierce wrote Eaton on September 4 that he was "baited and badgered . . . by creditors, lawyers, warrants, piratical bankers, and investigators." And on September 6 he wrote him again: "I don't propose to remain under fire very long, in a position which the circumstances of my own affairs have made peculiarly harassing and disagreeable, nor to hold that position by so insecure a tenure that I dare not send for my wife and babies. . . . Time presses, winter approaches and I mean to spend [it] with my family somewhere."[5] Yet in the face of incredible difficulties, he was so superbly efficient that "by the middle of September the great flume was within a mile of Rockerville, inching along and due to reach its goal."[6]

Walker's charges elicited a long rebuttal from Bierce and, on September 24, his formal resignation. He postponed his departure for three difficult weeks, however, until a successor could be appointed. During this time, with no money and with no official position, he had to ward off creditors and keep unpaid laborers working, while the capricious and inefficient Willsie took over temporarily. Miraculously, the company in early October washed a little gold in its own sluice boxes.

But Bierce, by now completely disenchanted, wanted to confront his accusers, explain his actions, launch a counterattack, and sever his connection with the company. On

October 16, therefore, he sent Shaler his "absolute and unconditional resignation" and left for New York, although Walker, his successor, had not yet arrived. Requesting Eddy Kaufman and Boone May to stay on the job until relieved, Bierce drew up his accounts, including over $50,000 of unpaid bills and $284.82 owing him based on a salary of $5,000 a year—his only reward after four months' backbreaking drudgery. Eaton sent him $500 for the trip to New York, where he stayed more than two months.

Walker went to Rockerville and took charge, but on December 1 the company was mortgaged for $50,000. The incompetent, dishonest Shaler, who was finally deposed, was replaced as president by Cornelius J. Vanderbilt, a large stockholder. The company careened crazily on for a few more months in the spring of 1881 under a succession of managers—one of them Bierce's father-in-law, Captain Day. But the smoldering volcano of lawsuits and debts on which it was precariously perched erupted and blew it apart that summer. The dam and flume were bought for $12,257.79; they produced water which was leased to mine owners, bringing prosperity to Rockerville until the rotting wooden flume began to disintegrate in the late 1880s. On December 30, 1882, Marcus Walker bought the defunct company in New York for $5.00. He never did anything with it, and it was dissolved in 1924.

Paul Fatout, in his exhaustive study of the Black Hills Placer Mining Company, has traced the later careers of prominent figures in this ill-starred enterprise. His findings cast light on the probable causes for the collapse of so promising a project. Shaler, who had an unsavory reputation in New York politics, barely escaped Sing Sing on charges of graft and corruption. West turned up in Mexico, living lavishly on credit, then skipped out leaving his debts unpaid. Fatout surmises that "the Black Hills Company was doomed from the moment West and Shaler met each other, before the treasurer ever handed over a dollar."[7]

Eaton's later career was one of integrity, but no record exists of continued friendship between him and Bierce. He became corporation counsel of what today is General Electric, and friend and adviser to Thomas Alva Edison. McGinnis continued as a successful broker.

Bierce himself had evidently planned, when the mine was firmly established, to settle permanently in Rockerville with his family. But this seemingly auspicious venture compensated him with only "that dubious asset, disillusioning experience." Although he obviously did not enjoy the fiasco and was later extraordinarily reticent about it, "he could have been gratified by the role he played. Even a good man may be defeated, and Bierce in the Hills was a good man. . . , skillful in business affairs, earnest, and devoted to a company that did not deserve his loyalty."[8] In Fatout's considered judgment, he was "the best businessman and the best miner in the company. Against odds that seem insuperable, he finished the job of building the flume, and he started it operating on the gravel bars."[9]

The bank case, however, dragged on. In September, 1881, attorneys McLaughlin and Steele, to whom it had been assigned by the company in default of paying them, got a long deposition from Bierce. Two years later, in the First District Court at Deadwood, the plaintiff, nominally Bierce although he had no interest in the suit, won after an eight-day trial. The verdict was appealed to the Supreme Court, which reversed the decision and charged Bierce costs of $400. He wanted to get out of the whole thing, but his friend Judge Boalt told him he was trapped in the litigation and legally liable. After a retrial in late 1885, won by the plaintiff, the verdict was again appealed. This time, however, in 1889, after nine weary years, the Supreme Court upheld it. McLaughlin and Steele collected their fee; and Bierce paid the costs, which were reduced to $213.

III *The* Wasp

On October 16, 1880, Bierce had left for New York, where he wound up his ill-fated connection with the Black Hills Placer Mining Company. In January, 1881, he returned to San Francisco, taking Mollie and the children to live in a rented house on a hillside overlooking the bay. He failed to get his old job on the *Argonaut* back; by March, however, he had secured the editorship of the weekly San Francisco *Wasp*, with which he was associated from 1881 to 1886, and a new phase of his career began. But his asthma continued to trouble him, and he spent most of his

time in Auburn, a small town in the foothills. He and his
friend E. L. G. Steele dabbled in various real-estate projects
in the surrounding area,[10] but nothing came of these; and
in 1886 Bierce moved his family to the village of St.
Helena in order to be near them.

The *Wasp*, in which he continued "Prattle" and started
in earnest *The Devil's Dictionary*, and where "What I Saw
of Shiloh" first appeared, followed as zigzag a course as
that of the Black Hills Placer Mining Company. However,
the publication offered Bierce a convenient outlet for
venting his wrath at the Central and Southern Pacific Railroads, which had seized control of California, dominating
not only the press but the state's corrupt politicians in
Washington as well as in Sacramento. He hounded these
feudal overlords, attacking "£eland $tanford" and his
vassal, Frank Pixley, Bierce's former boss on the *Argonaut*,
as well as numerous nonpolitical targets. But the *Wasp*'s
eventual owner, Ned Macfarlane, was too vacillating and
dependent to be successful in journalism. After a number
of embarrassing changes of policy, he sold the paper; and
Bierce in 1886 was once more out of a job.

CHAPTER 5

California Panjandrum

THE years between 1887 and 1899, the most significant of Bierce's life, were those of his greatest personal disasters but also his greatest journalistic and literary triumphs. Against the former—frail health, separation from his wife, and the tragic death of his elder son—his solace lay in stoicism: the Book of Job and Epictetus. Commenting on the therapeutic quality of Epictetus, he wrote: "When *I'm* in trouble and distress I read Epictetus. . . . It does not cure, but it helps one's endurance of the ill. I go to Epictetus with my mental malady as one consults one's family physician for one's physical—and misfortunes themselves are nothing except in so far as they affect us mentally."[1] The sense of tragedy and the deep compassion for the human condition which inspire his greatest stories undoubtedly owe something to Bierce's struggle against the fates. For, on the positive side, this period was his most productive one; it saw his journalistic triumphs on Hearst's *San Francisco Examiner* and *New York Journal*, his serious writing, and his acquisition of numerous friends and admirers.

I *The Bludgeonings of Destiny*

Although physically strong, Bierce continued to be plagued by strangling asthmatic attacks and insomnia, which today would probably be recognized as psychogenic and treated accordingly. Bierce's recourses, however, were flights to various little mountain resorts and desperate attempts to exhaust himself by hiking and cycling in the fresh outdoor air. His business activities centered around San Francisco, but he was able to live only briefly in that city or in Berkeley, Oakland, or San José. He stayed at various times in Auburn; in Sunol; in St. Helena; in Angwin, seven miles higher up on top of Howell Mountain; in Los Gatos, at the foot of the Santa Cruz range; or at

Wright's Station, above Los Gatos almost at the top of the Santa Cruz Mountains.

His living quarters tended to be in obscure small hotels, his solitude broken occasionally by visiting friends. Although dogs were anathema to him, many other species of pet (including those commonly scorned by most humans)— cats, squirrels, lizards, snakes, horned toads, chipmunks, rabbits, and birds—helped him while away the lonely hours. He had an astonishingly magnetic relationship with these little creatures, who would come to him during his hikes in the woods, sit trustingly on his arms and shoulders, or curl up in his pockets.

Cycling, one of his favorite recreations, was also a defense against ill health. He pedaled about the streets of Berkeley and Oakland or through pleasant country lanes, returning refreshed and invigorated. This pastime was temporarily interrupted by a serious accident he had in September, 1895, which invalided him for several weeks. Moreover, his chronic ailments were aggravated by two staggering crises. The first, his separation from Mollie, occurred about 1888, when he discovered some indiscreetly ardent love letters that a distinguished admirer had sent her. Though nothing seriously improper had occurred, a clue to the finality of Bierce's reaction may be found in a statement he made years later: "I never take part in any competition—not even for the favor of a woman."[2]

But even this calamity was surpassed by the one that succeeded it in July, 1889, when the sixteen-year-old Day was killed—along with his rival—in a gun duel over a girl in Chico, California. The stricken Ambrose came from Sunol, accompanied by Charlie Kaufman, to take his son's body to St. Helena for the funeral. Day's death under such violent circumstances was a terrible blow to Bierce; and, as was his wont, he reacted psychosomatically, being ill for weeks after the event.

Yet, as T. S. Eliot recognized, "History has many cunning passages, contrived corridors / And issues. . . . / She gives when our attention is distracted." And what she gave to Ambrose Bierce, in compensation for the personal tragedies darkening his life, was a concitation of his creative energies to produce those remarkable short stories on which, in large part, his literary reputation rests today. In a

tremendous burst of consummate art, he wrote, in rapid
succession, "One of the Missing"; "A Son of the Gods"; "A
Tough Tussle"; "Chickamauga"; "One Officer, One Man";
"A Horseman in the Sky"; "The Suitable Surroundings";
"The Affair at Coulter's Notch"; "A Watcher by the
Dead"; "The Man and the Snake"; "An Occurrence at Owl
Creek Bridge"; "Parker Adderson, Philosopher"; and "The
Death of Halpin Frayser." These stories were all first pub-
lished in ephemeral periodicals between March 11, 1888,
and December 25, 1891; and they are analyzed in consider-
able detail in Chapters 8 to 11 of this study.

The unconscious drives animating the creative imagination are of course the province of the psychologist rather
than the literary critic. Nevertheless, the conclusion seems
inescapable that the composition of these magnificent stories in such a concentrated span was in some sense a cathar-
tic activity for Bierce. That he had spent years of his life so
shaping and refining his technique that he had a ready in-
strument to hand when the time came to use it is something for which all connoisseurs of the short story have
cause to be grateful.

II *Journalistic Gladiator*

In the spring of 1887, moreover, Bierce had made his
most important professional connection when young
William Randolph Hearst lured him to the stellar staff of
the *San Francisco Examiner*, a powerful, respectable eight-
page daily.[3] Bierce, stipulating that "Prattle" was to appear
on the editorial page exactly as submitted, agreed to write
two columns for the Sunday edition, for which he would
be given a regular salary; but he was to do extra work at
space rates. With the resumption of "Prattle" in the *Examiner*, his Western influence and fame became enormous. Although he grew increasingly exasperated at the editors for
their carelessness in handling his copy and was continually
resigning and being enticed back, his association with
Hearst provided him with the two most interesting journalistic campaigns of his career: those involving the Southern
Pacific Railroad and the Spanish-American War.

By 1896 California politics was focused on a Funding
Bill, proposed by Pennsylvania's Congressman Reilly, which
would remit the enormous sums the railroads had borrowed

from the government. The Southern Pacific's president, Huntington, the only living member of the Big Four, was lobbying in Washington for the bill. But San Francisco, as well as the federal government (which stood to lose over a hundred and thirty million dollars), opposed it. The railroads, by varying freight rates according to an arbitrary commodity classification scheme, had a stranglehold on California businessmen, including those of the *Examiner*. And the strongest force against Reilly's bill was a Hearst lobby in Washington led by Bierce, who, accompanied by Leigh, had left California on January 20, 1896.

A struggle of titans ensued: on the one hand, Huntington and the railroad octopus; on the other, Bierce and the formidable minions of Hearst in Washington, San Francisco, and New York. Bierce, who favored government ownership of Western railroads, immediately began sending merciless dispatches from the capital which revealed Huntington's underhanded tactics. As each side sought political allies, the Hearst team applied so much pressure that friends of the Funding Bill decided it would be injudicious to press the measure in the House at the current session and the bill was routed, thanks largely to Bierce's efforts. The contest was postponed rather than finished, however; on April 25 Representative Powers of Vermont had introduced a second refunding bill that was to be debated at the next session.

Only a few days after Bierce had arrived in Washington, he also began writing editorials for the *New York Journal* (which Hearst had taken over in the autumn of 1895) as the opening gun in a battle between two newspaper tycoons: Hearst and Pulitzer (the *World* and *Sun*). Bierce continued to telegraph editorials to the *Journal* and to make frequent trips to New York while he was in Washington, for Hearst regarded Bierce's campaign against the Funding Bill as a special temporary mission. After its completion, Bierce planned to settle in New York with a regular department in the *Journal*, where Leigh already had a staff job.

But poor health and changes in the political scene caused Bierce to return to California in November, 1896, while Leigh remained in New York. When the Funding Bill was debated in the next session of Congress, Bierce was far from the conflict, although he made his sentiments known in "Prattle" on January 10, 1897. This bill, too, was defeated; the debt was then paid off in twenty semiannual installments, beginning on August 1, 1899, and ending on February 1, 1909.[4] Huntington's trickery, however, had made him fair game for blackmailers. In 1905, after his death, it was rumored that his widow had been mulcted of ten thousand dollars in a nefarious scheme disguised as a vanity writeup about her late husband.[5]

Through 1897-99 Bierce, though living in California, was writing for both the *San Francisco Examiner* and the *New York Journal*. But, by late summer, 1897, his relations with these publications were so precarious that he stopped writing "Prattle," saying that for "other stuff . . . they must outbid other fellows."[6] He even went so far as to try to surrender his seventy-five-dollar-a-week salary. Hearst, however, insisted on paying it, with Bierce working only when he felt like it and at what he pleased.

The major source of his dissatisfaction was the *Journal*. Both it and, occasionally, the *Examiner* were refusing to publish some of his best work. From his point of view, he was carrying on a one-man strike "and tranquilly pocketing [his] weekly wage," thinking he could hold out as long as Hearst. "It is a new kind of 'industrial combat' and I recommend it to the discontented 'toiler.' When the weekly check element is eliminated I shall go to work—for other papers."[7]

Then a new journalistic interest presented itself. As early as 1895 Bierce had remarked that "War—Horrid War!— between the United States and Spain has already broken out like a red rash in the newspapers."[8] He opposed it, contrary to the policy of both the *Journal* and the *Examiner*; Bierce, considering the war unnecessary and imperialistic, began his column "War Topics" to air his views. Before the war began, he wrote: "To all appearances . . . every demand that we have made upon Spain has been conceded . . . . It is difficult to discern . . . what is left to us to quarrel about."[9] Once the conflict had started, he satirized its romanticization; the assumption that the American position was supported by religion and morality; the military ignorance of reporters who transformed every incident into a "victory"; jingoistic patriotism; and the incompetence of American military and naval commanders.

On a more fundamental level, Bierce's analysis of the

significance of the war was astonishingly accurate in terms
of the future development of the United States and the
global violence of the twentieth century: "The passion for
territory once roused rages like a lion . . . . That is the fever
that is now burning in the American blood."[10] Predicting a
greatly enlarged navy, he foresaw the annexation of the
Philippines, Puerto Rico, and eventually Hawaii; America's
march toward world aggrandizement, he believed, had
begun. "Nations are like individuals: some are worthy of
liberty, others are not; and the same is true of peoples in
relation to their rulers. When asked if I am not an advocate
of liberty I ask in my turn: 'Whose liberty to do what?' "
And the terrifying developments of today are a grim commentary on his opinion that, ultimately, an airborne super-
bomb "whose detonation will reverberate around the
world" would sweep away forever "the entire set of pawns
and pieces."[11]

III *Litterateur*

During the period 1887-99 the early editions of Bierce's
most famous books—for the most part material from periodicals—were published. By September, 1890, he had collected a volume of his stories, which his friend E. L. G.
Steele published as *Tales of Soldiers and Civilians.* Andrew
Chatto paid Bierce fifty pounds for the rights to an English
edition, *In the Midst of Life*, giving it the magnificent title
by which the book is known today (from the burial service
in the Anglican Book of Common Prayer: "In the midst of
life we are in death"). Although the American edition bore
the date 1891, it was published simultaneously with the
English edition on January 28, 1892.[12]

Contrary to popular belief, the book was favorably received on both sides of the Atlantic, partly owing to the
clamorous publicity attending Gladstone's praise of a sec-
ond-hand copy of Bierce's twenty-year-old *The Fiend's
Delight.* Readers and reviewers, who prophesied the new
book's eventual success, ranked Bierce with Hawthorne and
Poe, and urged him to publish a French translation. He
developed epistolary friendships with the young English-
born Walter Blackburn Harte, co-editor of the Boston *New
England Magazine*, who died in the summer of 1899; Percival Pollard; and Brander Matthews, who had reviewed the

book favorably in *Cosmopolitan*. Bierce's fame, indeed, grew to such proportions as to attract the attention of Hamlin Garland; and William Dean Howells, who always had a kindly attitude toward emerging talent, referred to him as one of the six leading men of letters in America.

Nevertheless, with few exceptions Bierce's dealings with publishers during this period were disastrous. Late in 1892, the plates of the American edition of *Soldiers and Civilians* were sent to the United States Publishing Company in New York in a doomed effort to bring the book out in the East. The company failed, with large liabilities; and in February, 1896, all its business was turned over to the American Publishers Corporation. By October, this firm had sold some copies of *Tales of Soldiers and Civilians*, but it too went bankrupt within a few months.

Meanwhile, other publishing projects were going on. Late in 1890 a young German-Jewish dentist, Dr. Gustav Adolph Danziger, with whom Bierce had been on friendly terms, read a story by Richard Voss, *Der Mönch von Berchtesgaden*, in the German monthly *Vom Fels Zum Meer*. Danziger made a rough translation and then signed an agreement with Bierce on June 18, 1891, to publish the story serially in the *Examiner* and in book form.

The conditions of the agreement were as follows: (1) Bierce, who knew no German, was to rewrite the story from Danziger's manuscript; (2) it was to be published "with the names of G. A. Danziger and Ambrose Bierce jointly on the title page as adapters"; (3) Danziger was "to assume all expenses of publication and advertising"; (4) two-thirds of the book profits were to go to Danziger; one-third, to Bierce; (5) two-thirds of the newspaper profits were to go to Bierce; one-third, to Danziger; (6) Danziger was to pay Bierce fifty dollars a week, up to an amount not exceeding two hundred dollars, while Bierce was doing the rewriting; (7) Bierce was to repay this money from his share of the profits of publication.[13]

The result of this collaboration, *The Monk and the Hangman's Daughter*, quickly became a bone of contention over which the adapters snarled for years. The work began to appear in the *Examiner* on September 13, 1891, with a by-line crediting it to "Dr. G. A. Danziger and Ambrose Bierce"; then, in 1892, F. J. Schulte of Chicago published it as a handsome book in an edition of six thousand copies. Danziger, who was constantly making trouble over both versions, finally asserted that Bierce owed him two hundred dollars for the *Examiner* translation and claimed ownership of the book copyright. To the first charge Bierce angrily responded: "You had not only 'your share from the publication in the *Examiner*,' but my share too. The story brought $199.00. You took it all and I hold your receipts for every cent of it." To the second he retorted: "I have a one-third interest in the copyright of that book . . . ; you are bound by the contract."[14]

Danziger, who also showed a paranoid fear of being "robbed" by Schulte, tried to extort money from Bierce; but he finally conceded, with ill grace, that the senior author was entitled to his one-third share of the profits from the book. Unfortunately, Schulte's firm shortly collapsed, and neither Danziger nor Bierce got a cent. Both took credit for the novella's literary value. Frank Monaghan, however, on the basis of an exhaustive comparison of their version with Voss's German original, claims that the only changes made were unimportant deletions and additions, plus an ironic conclusion. "The rest . . . is either close paraphrasing or literal translation."[15]

The Monk and the Hangman's Daughter was not the only cause of controversy. Danziger and a William M. Langton, who had formed a shaky vanity enterprise, the Western Authors Publishing Company, had persuaded Bierce to advance them five hundred dollars. In return, in 1892 the "company" brought out *Black Beetles in Amber*, a volume of Bierce's satirical verse whose title was probably inspired by Walter Blackburn Harte's disappointment at his "spinning amber round stinking fish."[16] Against Bierce's advice, Danziger, as Langton's agent, had handled the costs of publication, over which he squabbled so vociferously that the exasperated author finally insisted on severing his business connection with Danziger and Langton. Accordingly, in October, 1894, Danziger signed a notarized agreement relinquishing to Bierce all rights in *Black Beetles in Amber* on behalf of himself and Langton.

Bierce's friends had long criticized his satire because it dealt with inconsequential figures, an objection that interfered with plans for commercial publication of the book.

Stone and Kimball, a new firm in Cambridge, wanted to publish a selection from it; but they hesitated because the beetles were such minor insects. Bierce's reply not only closed the negotiations but illuminates his theory of satire:

> If the obscurity (in the East) of the persons satirized is a fatal objection no considerable selection can be made. It does not appear to be an objection in such works as the "English Bards and Scotch Reviewers," "The Dunciad," and most of the satires which have lived; but of course I am not a Byron nor a Pope. Nevertheless, I cannot see how the quality or interest of a piece is affected by application to a real, though unknown, person instead of presenting it as a general satire, with perhaps a fictitious name. If the verse is good it *makes* the victims known; if not good it is not worth publishing anyhow.[17]

Meanwhile, under Steele's guidance, another collection of short stories was being published by Cassell and Company of New York. It bore a splendid title—*Can Such Things Be?*—based on a passage referred to many years earlier in *Nuggets and Dust*, from *Macbeth*, III, iv, ll. 110-12: "Can such things be,/And overcome us like a summer's cloud,/Without our special wonder?" But, after Bierce had read about three-fourths of the proofs, Cassell's embezzling manager absconded. Nevertheless, the moribund company gave a few convulsive gasps, and the book appeared in December, 1893. That summer, however, the faithful and industrious Steele died; and Bierce, dissatisfied with the bookkeeping of the company, which he felt prevented him from accounting adequately to Steele's heirs, complained to the American Authors' Guild.

Bierce had been unfortunate indeed in his publishers, most of whom had failed: F. J. Schulte (*The Monk and the Hangman's Daughter*), the United States Book Company and the American Publishers Corporation (*Tales of Soldiers and Civilians*), the Western Authors Publishing Company (*Black Beetles in Amber*), and Cassell (*Can Such Things Be?*). Commenting wryly that each of his books brought down "a publisher[']s gray hair in sorrow to the grave!" Bierce claimed "a fairly good array of notches in [his] rifle-stock."[18] But the succession of bankruptcies was so traumatic an experience that he henceforth viewed the whole tribe with a jaundiced eye.

Yet his luck was shortly to turn. Edward S. Kaufman, handling Bierce's affairs in New York City, persuaded G. P. Putnam's Sons to publish a revised and enlarged edition of *In the Midst of Life*. When it appeared in 1898, it earned favorable reviews and a few dollars in royalties; Chatto and Windus also issued a new edition in 1898. Then Leigh Bierce negotiated a second contract with Putnam's for *Fantastic Fables*, published in 1899; and Bierce sent his son a volume of verse in manuscript, *Shapes of Clay* (a title suggested by Gertrude Atherton taken from *The Rubáiyát*) to submit to New York publishers.

IV   *The Balm of* Φιλία

During these years of flurried activity, Bierce found much consolation among his numerous friends and admirers: Carrie Christiansen, Ina and Frederick Peterson, Jeremiah Lynch, Charlie and Eddy Kaufman, Joaquin Miller, E. L. G. Steele, and many others. Bierce met the diffident young Carrie Christiansen at Angwin before his separation from Mollie. His entire family befriended her, and he sent her to normal school at Berkeley. She became a schoolteacher and eventually began to act as his nurse, secretary, and general Girl Friday, at first in California and, years later, in Washington.

Moreover, he was acquiring a special category of friends and protégés: his "pupils," fledgling writers who sent him their manuscripts for criticism and made pilgrimages to his out-of-the-way living quarters. Although a terror to bad poets, Bierce was often kind to aspiring beginners. "We all have our favorite recreations," he wrote; "mine is helping young writers who do not immodestly and presumptuously 'rush in where angels fear to tread.' "[19]

The most interesting of these young writers was probably Gertrude Atherton, who sent him a manuscript which he criticized. When he wrote that he had been trying unsuccessfully to conjure up her image, she responded: "I am a tearing beauty, of course. I wonder you had not heard it before."[20] She soon visited him at Sunol, and the two carried on an extensive correspondence involving a tacit mutual-assistance pact for many years. His half, unfortunately, is no longer extant. But, if one can judge from her side, his letters to her must rank among the most delightful he ever penned. Nearly always charming in writing to women, he found in Mrs. Atherton someone of the opposite sex as gay, witty, and irreverent as he himself. She kept an eye on his interests in New York, where she moved in 1892, and in London, where she sailed in 1895. For his part, in "Prattle" for September 23, 1894, he commented favorably on her new book of short stories, *Before the Gringo Came*, and "her incomparable *Doomswoman*." Then he added: "Since the suicide of Richard Realf gave us that noble crown of sonnets on the event, the successive appearances of Mrs. Atherton's books—with a few poems by Joaquin Miller—appear to me about all that has occurred having a claim to Californian attention." In "Prattle" for October 13, 1895, he wrote a long review praising her novel, *A Whirl Asunder*, particularly the heroine.

Bierce and Gertrude Atherton not only shared an interest in writing but in many mutual friends, including Elodie Hogan, who married the young Hilaire Belloc after a fevered six-year courtship on June 16, 1896. The Bellocs left San Francisco to settle in England, but Mrs. Atherton kept Bierce posted on the progress of the union.

Another "pupil" was Edwin Markham, whose early poems Bierce criticized and admired. Then, at a New Year's Eve party in 1899, Markham read "The Man with the Hoe," which Bailey Millard promptly praised in the *Examiner* for January 15. Bierce, however, detested the poem; and he subjected it to a barrage of critical attack in the *Examiner* throughout 1899 for its demagogic emphasis on class warfare and its artistic flaws. (E. C. Stedman, whose critical ability Bierce respected, pointed out the same flaws.) As Markham began fancying himself an authority on social and economic questions, relations gradually cooled between him and Bierce.

Other "pupils" who achieved some fame were George Sterling, George Herman Scheffauer, W. C. Morrow, Charles William Doyle, and John Herbert Evelyn Partington and his daughter Blanche. Sterling and Scheffauer were young poets on whose literary efforts Bierce expended many hours of critical labor; although their dependency on him was well publicized, he eventually lost patience with both. Dr. Doyle was a popular and fashionable English physician of Santa

Cruz. The Partingtons Bierce regarded as the most interesting family he knew. The father was a talented English painter who exhibited a prize-winning oil portrait of Bierce at the 1893 San Francisco World's Fair. This painting the artist later gave to Helen Bierce, who had moved to Los Angeles with her mother. Partington also tried his hand at writing, and even planned, with his subject's cooperation, a biography of Bierce, although it never materialized. One of the artist's accomplished children, Blanche, wanted also to write; and Bierce tried to help her. He sent her long, encouraging letters, telling her what books to read, criticizing her manuscripts, and warning her against debasing her talent by using it for reform. His friendship with her was at its height in the early 1890s.

But his most poignant tutorials were with an underprivileged young deaf woman, Elizabeth (Lily) Walsh, who aspired to become a writer. Motivated by admiration for Bierce's towering position as literary dictator of the West Coast, she sent him, in January, 1895, a poem, signed "Tip-Tilt," followed by several misspelled and rather ungrammatical missives. Although she was twenty-three years old, her letters had a curiously childlike quality which probably appealed to Bierce. In February, he wrote her, frankly, but tactfully and kindly, criticizing her verses and suggesting that she repair the gaps in her education before attempting to become a poet. She responded to his friendly encouragement and advice with overwhelming devotion.

Feeling that she was handicapped by lack of schooling, he got her into an institution for educating the deaf, dumb, and blind at Berkeley on August 28, 1895. But she had been there only one day when an acute fever struck her down. As her illness dragged on for almost a month, it became clear that she could not improve sufficiently to attend classes; eventually, she was transferred to the Fabiola Hospital, Oakland, where she died on October 20, 1895. Bierce rushed to her bedside, but it was too late.

To his disappointment, her expressed wish to be buried at Los Gatos near him was not fulfilled; since her relatives were Catholics, her body was interred in St. Mary's Cemetery at Oakland. Bierce undertook to beautify her grave, however, with grass and flowers, a granite curbing, and a simple granite headstone on which he wanted to put a wittily pathetic epitaph she had written. Although her brother Myles approved, the cemetery officials did not; the only inscription was, therefore, "Lily Walsh / 1872-1895."

But, as Bierce's fame spread, the character of his friendships altered. Although he never completely lost interest in helping young writers, his literary output was attracting readers and reviewers who concentrated on his work instead of seeking advice about their own. The critic Percival Pollard was an important member of this group.

Bierce had stopped off in Chicago to see Pollard on his way east in January, 1896, and their friendship bloomed. Pollard considered Stephen Crane "an imitation of Bierce." Writing in the *New York Journal* for May 22, 1896, he attacked *The Red Badge of Courage*, commenting "that Mr. Crane had merely done crudely what Bierce had done admirably." He defied anyone to "show a passage in *The Red Badge of Courage* 'so vividly and truly descriptive of the wounded crawling over a battlefield' as that in Bierce's 'Chickamauga.' "[21] Bierce, who promptly responded, wrote Pollard: "That was a pleasant reminder of your continued existence that you gave me in The Journal, and my sense of it is lively. I valued it, I really believe, more for its just censure of the Crane freak than for its too kindly praise of me."[22] The Prattler then attacked Crane publicly in the *Examiner* on July 26, 1896.

V *The Beckoning East*

As the years wore on, many of Bierce's California ties loosened; by August, 1897, he was contemplating a return to the East. The new friends he was making were not Californians; and many of his old ones had either died, left the state, or weakened their relationship with him. Moreover, Leigh, now twenty-four, was still in New York, a reporter for the *Journal* and acting as his father's Eastern agent. And Percival Pollard, with whom Bierce was in close touch, had moved from Chicago to Saybrook, Connecticut. In late November, 1899, Bierce wrote: "In a few weeks I expect to go to Washington, D.C., where I shall probably remain. It is simply a change of residence without a change of duties, excepting that I shall probably do more work for 'The Journal' and less for 'The Examiner.' "[23] Accordingly, he left San Francisco on December 12, 1899.

The *Examiner* for December 14 reported in a send-off article that Bierce was being sent to the capital to report on the Fifty-sixth Congress' disposition of "such matters as the war in the Philippines, the adjustment of our new colonial policy, the disposition of Cuban affairs, our foreign relations, particularly with England and Germany, and, what is possibly most vital of all, the action that Congress may or may not take with reference to the trusts." Then the article cautiously stated: "While Mr. Bierce's work is necessarily editorial in its tone, he does not always reflect 'The Examiner's' opinions or policy. There have been many instances in which he has violently opposed this paper's well-known ideas side by side with them on the editorial page." Henceforth, Bierce lived in the East until his last long hegira into oblivion.

CHAPTER 6

The Poise of an Olympian

BIERCE'S last thirteen years saw the consolidation of his literary position, increased nostalgia for his Civil War days, the refinement of his stoicism to a serene philosophy of detachment, and his mysterious disappearance—the most dramatic departure from life of any American man of letters. Although his nemesis continued to hound him, in the East his health improved greatly. His strangulating attacks of asthma and influenza were infrequent, and enough documentation exists to demonstrate their psychological origin. A recital of the traumata preceding each of his physiological reactions makes clear that, although he managed to preserve an outward semblance of equanimity in the face of each blow, his body cried out in torment afterward.

Leigh Bierce had married in 1900. Like Ambrose, he had a long history of bronchial ailments; and on March 31, 1901, he died of pneumonia in New York. His father spent two anguished weeks at his bedside before returning to Washington. Then Helen, who had come from Los Angeles for an extended visit, fell ill with typhoid fever and was hospitalized for eight weeks. She recovered and in December returned to Los Angeles; but Bierce, who had been terrified lest he lose his one remaining child, suffered from asthma throughout this period. When she was divorced from her first husband in 1906, Bierce reacted with hives.

On April 27, 1905, Mollie, who had only recently divorced him, died of heart disease in Los Angeles. Bierce, reticent as usual about his personal griefs, wrote Sterling on May 16, 1905: "Death has been striking pretty close to me again, and you know how that upsets a fellow."[1] Significantly, in the summer of 1905 he was again seriously ill.

In 1909, while correcting the proofs of *In the Midst of Life* (a work in which he had drowned the pain of Day's death by recalling the agony of the Civil War), he suffered a relapse. And in 1911, after a summer at Sag Harbor in which he was treated with scant courtesy by George Sterling, the protégé on whom he had lavished so much attention, he had yet another. In 1912, on his return from a disappointing trip to northern California, he was sick in bed for almost a month. In 1913, having completed his last extensive tour of his old battlefields, he was ill again.

I *Years of Contentment*

But, on the whole, Bierce led a prosperous and satisfying life. When he first went to Washington, he was on the payroll of the *New York Journal* at a hundred dollars a week; but his material also appeared in the *New York American* and the *San Francisco Examiner*. His relations with the Hearst papers were very uneasy, however, and in 1906 he resigned permanently because of the way their editors mangled and distorted his work. Hearst's *Cosmopolitan*, for which he continued to write, then paid his salary. But editorial control of the magazine was so unstable that in 1909, having begun the compilation of his *Collected Works*, he resigned from it, putting the blame (at last) squarely on Hearst instead of on his editors.

He was helped in maintaining his tranquility by his hobbies—cycling, hiking, canoeing, cooking and gourmandizing, playing billiards, coddling his pets. He also acquired a circle of congenial cronies, with whom he spent many happy hours. Shortly after he moved to Washington, he became a prominent member of the Army and Navy Club; and among his closest associates were high-ranking officers with whom he shot billiards and discussed military affairs; he even contributed a uniform system of giving oral commands. His Civil War brevet title was revived, and during his Washington years he was known as Major Bierce.

Moreover, Carrie Christiansen had followed him east, secured a teaching job in Washington, and settled in at his apartment building, the Olympia, shortly after his own installation there. Her devoted ministrations contributed greatly to the ease and contentment of his last years. No indication exists that she was Bierce's mistress; instead, she played the role of companion, nurse, secretary, confidante, and traveling associate—always carefully chaperoned, frequently by one or two of her fellow schoolteachers. Bierce, indeed, called these women "middle-aged innocents," and the probability is that, in sexual matters at least, they were. And he had several close literary friends—most notably Silas Orrin Howes, a young Texas newspaperman who compiled and edited a collection of his essays entitled *The Shadow on the Dial*; Pollard, the critic and travel writer, with whom Bierce fraternized on frequent holiday trips; H. L. Mencken, whom he found very congenial; and Walter Neale, a publisher many years his junior who began to take an interest in his output. Bierce began acquiring copyright control of his various books, and in 1906 Neale proposed a collected edition of his work that was to be published by subscription.

II *The* Collected Works

Although the subscription angle had little appeal for Bierce, he did want to leave a permanent monument to his literary endeavors. Consequently, he signed a contract with Neale, and embarked upon the herculean chore of preparing his *Collected Works*. From 1908 to 1912 his labors were concentrated on this task; indeed, these were probably the busiest years of his entire life. The original plan had been to publish a ten-volume set, but this was expanded to twelve by adding Howes's book as Volume XI, *Antepenultimata*, and a collection of miscellaneous material, including the Little Johnny essays, as Volume XII, *In Motley*.

III *Contentious Associates*

Some mention should be made of Bierce's relations with three people who continued to trade on their friendship with him for the rest of their lives, and to whom—since they all discussed it extensively—many of the misinterpretations of his character can be traced: George Sterling, Herman Scheffauer, and Danziger (later Adolphe de Castro). Of all these associations, the most attention has been paid to that with Sterling. Since it has been greatly exaggerated, it is time to set the record straight. To begin with, it was very one-sided; a sympathetic older man of letters encouraged a young protégé, and the advantages accrued to Ster-

ling. Theirs was primarily a literary and not a personal relationship, for the two men were far apart in temperament.
Bierce had an innate sensitivity in comparison with
which Sterling seems rather coarse-grained (when Percival
Pollard died horribly after a brain operation in December,
1911, Sterling wrote the grief-stricken Bierce a tactless,
joking letter). Bierce was sturdily independent; Sterling,
narcissistic, egocentric, clinging. Reading over their correspondence, one gets the impression of a parasitic vine wrap-
ping itself about a stalwart oak; until the last year of their
correspondence, Sterling, overriding Bierce's objections,
addressed him as "Magister" or "Master." Bierce was un-
mercenary to a degree, yet he understood the necessity for
earning a living, and he was a good businessman. Sterling,
in spite of the bohemianism he flaunted, appears crass in
his attitude toward money, rather like a child who feels
that he is entitled to an allowance all his life simply because he exists. Bierce, incorruptible in his personal relationships, preserved a decent reticence about them; Sterling
at times came perilously close to insincerity, and his confi-
dences about his wife and his mistress Bierce regarded as
appallingly candid.

From 1900 to 1908 Sterling's literary dependence on
Bierce was at its height. He bombarded the older man with
letters pleading for advice about his poetry and about
points of grammar and prosody. Bierce responded generously, but he maintained by 1909 that Sterling had passed his
apprentice period and needed no further criticism. There
had been friction between them as early as 1904 when
Bierce had discovered that his *Shapes of Clay*, whose "publication" in San Francisco in 1903 had been arranged by
Sterling, was in reality a vanity deal for which Sterling had
secretly advanced seven hundred dollars. Bierce, who insisted on paying back the money, was extremely annoyed
at having been saddled with a debt which it took him years
to liquidate.

For a time Sterling had a job with Frank C. Havens, his
millionaire uncle, in a realty syndicate. He hated the disciplined life, but it was his most productive period. Then in
1905 he moved to beautiful Carmel-by-the-Sea, which he
tried to establish as a writers' and artists' colony. Although
he continued to work sporadically and reluctantly for his

uncle, he tended to settle happily down to a bohemian life, swimming, hiking, shellfishing, womanizing, and drinking; and he spent less and less time on actual writing. More irritating to Bierce was Sterling's attempt to involve his mentor with his own friends—notably Jack London, whose Socialism Bierce deplored; Herman Scheffauer, with whom Bierce had broken off; and even Sterling's mistress.

On a summer trip to California in 1910, Bierce saw a good deal of Sterling and his crowd, but their social philosophies were radically different, and Bierce did not enjoy the meetings. Moreover, although Sterling basked in his friendship with the famous older writer, he misrepresented Bierce's views to others and made invidious comments about him, some of which eventually reached Bierce. From this time on, Sterling treated Bierce with scant courtesy. Although each time they had a difference, it was patched up, and although they spent some weeks together in Sag Harbor in the summer of 1911, the tie was clearly neither deep nor close.

Extremely disillusioning to Bierce was Sterling's failure, after years of loudly proclaiming his admiration, to subscribe to the *Collected Works*. When, in 1912, Sterling at last bought a cheap twenty-five-dollar edition of the twelve volumes, Bierce wrote him: "So—you[']ve subscribed for the Collected Works. Good!—that is what you ought to have done a long time ago."[2] In 1912, when Bierce returned to California, he continued to be annoyed at Sterling's fawning and insincere behavior and refused an invitation to Carmel. A year later he wrote a friend: "I never hear from Sterling and his entourage of social impossibles; there is not enough charitableness in this vale of tears to make them and me personally congenial, or even compatible."[3]

Herman Scheffauer was another young protégé who capitalized on his friendship with Bierce. In 1904 the two made a trip to New York and Saybrook, Connecticut (where Percival Pollard lived). Scheffauer, who then toured Europe and North Africa, bombarded Bierce with postcards and with long letters bragging about his conquests of women, some of whom the older man knew and respected. Mightily offended, he cut off the correspondence; by 1906 his relations with Scheffauer had collapsed. In 1907 the two were reconciled after Scheffauer promised to change for the better. But a second, and permanent, break occurred in 1908-09 when the "new" Scheffauer denigrated Bierce's critical ability to Sterling and Walter Neale, both of whom passed on his aspersions.

And, finally, Bierce's relations with Danziger, who had settled in New York, continued stormy. In 1900-01 the penniless little dentist tried to worm his way back into favor. When he grew very sick, Bierce gave him some money, paid his bills, and intervened with California Congressman Julius Kahn to get him a consulship. After Danziger recovered, he departed for Europe. While there, he signed an agreement on March 23, 1902, at Chateau Renault, France, turning over all rights in *The Monk and the Hangman's Daughter* to Bierce. But, when Danziger returned to New York in July, he found Bierce very angry, not only because of unsettled bills he had left behind which Bierce had paid, but also because he had attempted to borrow money from Bierce's friends in Europe. Although Danziger was very downcast, Bierce said flatly that their relationship henceforth must be a strictly commercial one.

In 1907 Neale republished *The Monk* in an edition of five hundred copies. Danziger exploded, saying that he owned the copyright (a claim he continued to make for the rest of his life); but, since it had long since been transferred to Bierce, Neale rightly treated his threats as a bluff.

IV *Holidays*

During his Washington residency, one of Bierce's favorite recreations was traveling. Besides frequent jaunts to New York, Baltimore, and other places not far from Washington, he took an extended vacation each summer or fall, including visits to Civil War sites in 1903 and 1907, to Galveston (with Percival Pollard) in 1907, and to Sag Harbor in 1911. The most significant trips, however, were the two he made to California in 1910 and 1912. He had been much distressed by the San Francisco earthquake of 1906, and even that early he had feared the city he knew and loved would never reappear. But the changes went far deeper than mere rebuilding. Although he looked forward to his holidays with enthusiasm, they were not really successful, for he disliked the "false fool gods"[4] which fascinated his California relatives and friends: Socialism, which he opposed, although he thought its coming was inevitable; anarchism; Christian Science; uninhibited sexual attitudes; women's suffrage; and the dominance of labor unions. He spent most of his time with his brother Albert, his nephew Carleton, Carlt's wife Lora, and the Sterlings. Many other demands were made on him, however, for he was by now a literary lion of roaring eminence, and he spent much time and effort avoiding excessive and rather superficial socializing. These two expeditions completed his disillusionment with California and in particular with Carmel's literary colony, which he regarded as an untalented group of bohemians. The first trip, however, did give him an opportunity to see what he regarded as "the three greatest things of this continent—the Grand Cañon, Yosemite and the work on the Panama Canal."[5]

V *One of the Missing*

By the fall of 1912, the *Collected Works* completed, Bierce's thoughts were turning to his last long rest. He wrote numerous letters outlining his plans. After a preliminary tour of his old Civil War battlefields, he intended to cross the border from Texas into Mexico (where Pancho Villa was leading a popular rebellion against the reactionary government of General Victoriano Huerta), join Villa's forces as an observer, and proceed eventually to South America.

It would be an oversimplification to say that Bierce meant to commit suicide on his forthcoming trip; on the other hand, he clearly believed that he might not return. In early 1913, when he transferred a California cemetery lot to Helen, he said he did "not wish to lie there. That matter is all arranged, and you will not be bothered about the mortal part of/Your Daddy."[6] A few months later, in letters to two friends, he wrote: "Bah! I'd hate to die between sheets, and, God willing, I won't."[7]

My plan, so far as I have one, is to go through Mexico to one of the Pacific ports, if I can *get* through without being stood up against a wall and shot as an American. Thence I hope to sail for some port in South America. Thence go across the

Andes and perhaps across the continent . . . . Naturally, it is
possible—even probable—that I shall not return. These be
"strange countries," in which things happen; that is why I am
going. And I am seventy-one![8]

His movements can be traced with great exactitude until
December 26, 1913. He left Washington on October 2,
1913; and, after touring the sites where he had fought in
the Civil War, he arrived about October 24 in New Orleans,
where he was laid up for a few days with asthma. There he
granted lengthy interviews to three reporters, discussing his
retirement as a writer and his plans to reach South America. From October 27 to November 5, he was in San Anto-
nio, Texas, again suffering from asthma. On November 7 he
reached Laredo, Texas, where he stayed until November 10,
visiting the United States soldiers at Fort McIntosh and the
Mexican Federals across the Rio Grande at Nuevo Laredo,
which was held by the Huertistas.

From Laredo, Bierce went to El Paso; thence to Juarez,
which Villa had captured on November 15. In Juarez he
was given credentials to accompany Villa's army, and went
to Chihuahua, which Villa occupied on December 8. His
last letter, December 26, 1913, states that he intended to
go from Chihuahua to Ojinaga the next day. General Tori-
bio Ortega led part of the Villista forces from Chihuahua
City a hundred and twenty-five miles northeast to Ojinaga
(on the Rio Grande almost opposite Presidio, Texas), which
they besieged for ten days, beginning on January 1, 1914.
On January 7, Ortega was joined by Villa. Ojinaga was
captured on January 11, 1914, after a fierce battle at
whose conclusion all the corpses were piled in heaps and
burned to prevent the spread of typhus. Salvador Ibarra,
one of General Ortega's officers, recalled seeing Bierce
going into the battle, but not afterward. Captain Emil
Holmdahl, another rebel officer, heard later that "an old
gringo" had been shot during the fighting.

Although the evidence is circumstantial, to my mind, at
least, there is no doubt that Bierce was killed in the battle
of Ojinaga on January 11, 1914. He had made no mystery
of his plans; the passages I have quoted represent only a
fraction of the voluminous correspondence he maintained
until December 26, 1913. All his life he was a conscien-

tious letter writer; the last few months were no exception, and he kept many people posted on every step of his itinerary. [He was, as he had pointed out, seventy-one years old. And he was an asthmatic. While I do not believe that he was technically a suicide, he was a brave man and I suspect made no particular effort to safeguard himself during this bloody battle.]

Certainly Walter Neale and Carrie Christiansen behaved as if he were dead. Neale, who had always been a little overawed by the much stronger personality of Bierce, had treated his star author with so much circumspection as to induce him to purchase considerable stock in the company. But early in 1914 Neale began reneging on both royalty and dividend payments to Carrie Christiansen, Bierce's heiress. The despairing Miss Christiansen cited to no avail written agreements between Bierce and Neale; all income to her from the Neale Publishing Company soon ceased. After her death, Neale published a biography of Bierce in which he made many innuendoes about her relationship with its subject—innuendoes which a careful examination of much personal correspondence convinces me had no basis in fact.

CHAPTER 7

Growth of the Artist

BIERCE'S compelling personality and the enigma of his disappearance have obscured close analysis of his writings. Yet in a very real—though not obviously apparent —sense, knowledge of his life contributes to understanding developments in his art. An examination of these developments furnishes a background for the more detailed examination of specific works.

I *The Flower Driven Through the Green Fuse*

When he was sixty-four, Bierce cast a retrospective glance at his work on the *Argonaut*: "I was a slovenly writer in those days, though enough better than my neighbors to have attracted my own attention. My knowledge of English was imperfect 'a whole lot.' Indeed, my intellectual status (whatever it may be, and God knows it's enough to make me blush) was of slow growth—as was my moral. I mean, I had not literary sincerity."[1]

The point here, genetically related to his technique, is that Bierce laboriously worked out for himself not only such mechanical matters as spelling, grammar, and the acquisition of a ready vocabulary for communicating exactly what he wanted to say, but also his view of man and the universe. An aristocrat in tastes, he had taken for his masters the aristocrats of literature: the great classics. Unlike Benjamin Franklin, he left no record of how he learned his craft. But, like Franklin, he was self-taught. Accordingly, he had learned the hard way that constant self-criticism is necessary on the far from royal road to learning.

It is thus no accident that Bierce did not create his finest work until he was middle-aged. There was no sudden reversal in his career, like the dramatic turnabout in Walt Whitman's; for the creative potential was present in him from childhood, and was developed slowly over the years. As has been indicated in this study, certain elements in his craftsmanship and certain ideas in his philosophy appeared very soon. Even the misspelled journal passage of his early twenties describing his trip to Panama reveals sharpness of observation and a flair for words. And the apprentice writings that attained a kind of permanence in the London books of 1873 and 1874 he held in such contempt show not only these qualities but the characteristic self-reliance and audacity which were to broaden into a studied insistence on reexamining every received opinion on its merits. Thus Bierce discovered that things are not often what they seem. If fools and rogues were taken in by surface appearances, so be it; his well-known mockery and irony revealed them for what they were. Reality lay deeper, and he who dug with his own spade could find it. Because Bierce's education was autodidactic, it was unceasing and resulted in a continuous deepening of his philosophy and sharpening of his technique. He habitually revised his work through successive editions, always for the purpose of clarifying or refining some point on which his own thinking had advanced.

II *The Existential Moment*

Bierce had learned that man stands poised precariously on the abyss of anguish, despair, and death. Most critical human actions are motivated at those junctures when the soul is stripped naked and, for better or worse, stands alone. These crucial moments in a man's—or a woman's—life are those which not only indicate the pattern of his personality, but reveal his character.

Thus even the man who is able to strike through the mask to the reality beyond finds himself, in a moment of crisis, faced with the ultimate existential anxiety. As a living, sentient organism he *must* act, with such awareness and such understanding as he can muster of forces that are frequently dark and mysterious. Involved are not only his own being, but also history, human nature, and, finally, the universe itself. How he will act—or react—at such moments is a terrifying self-revelation, for in the last analysis it is himself alone on whom he must rely. His best is often not good enough, and he may plunge into the abyss. The solitary confrontation, however, with the desert places of nature, the cosmos, and his inner being he cannot avoid. When he faces it, he may not recover. But during that stark agony, as at no other time, he discovers who he is, what life is, what it means to be. If he lives at all after that—and he may not—he will, like Young Goodman Brown, never again be the same.

III *The Quest for Forms*

To convey such a philosophy certain kinds of works are clearly more appropriate than others. The novel had little appeal for Bierce; he thought the short story was much superior to it as a literary form. And it is easy to understand why. It was the sudden, sharp crisis that interested him. This crisis reveals the man for what he is; his past life is important only for what it contributes to this critical juncture. Obviously a writer of narrative prose fiction will find the short story far better suited to portraying this climactic kind of incident than the novel, with its slow accretion of detail.

Bierce's distaste for the novel and his preference for the short story are, accordingly, perfectly consistent with what he was trying to do. The short story may demonstrate a general principle or portray a limited segment of life. But whichever it does, it works within a narrow compass. It cannot develop a plot on the grand scale as the novel does. But at its best what it can do superlatively well is to distill the core of an idea or the essence of a crisis. It can place the brief span of action it represents under a microscope, as it were, to magnify it and show the reader its significance. And just as the microscopic examination of a single cell can tell us something about all similar cells, so a study of Bierce's best short stories about the crises individual men face can tell us something about all men. Such stories, like much lyric poetry—Emily Dickinson comes to mind—have universal implications for humanity.

But there are dangers. The novelist can make mistakes that the short story writer dare not make. In the novel, an episode or two which is out of key with the work as a whole need not necessarily ruin it. But the short story, since it is confined to only a few episodes—perhaps even a single incident—can be destroyed by a blemish which would pass unnoticed in the novel. A few sentences, a single sentence, sometimes even a phrase or a word which jars with the rest of the story can cause the neutralization or collapse of the effect the writer is aiming at. Bierce did not always avoid this danger, particularly in his early career. "A Working Girl's Story," for example, one of the tales in his 1873 *Nuggets and Dust*, develops a tone of genuine pathos which is spoiled by the abrupt intrusion of the comic. Bierce was not perfect—no author is. Occasional lapses of taste are found in his writing, and when they occur, because he worked in the shorter forms, they are glaring.

A writer is not memorable for his failures, however, but for his successes. And Bierce, at his best, was a consummate craftsman. The key to his technique is that it compresses much in narrow compass. He was master of a fluid and limpid prose, often intentionally ambivalent, in which exactly the right words are chosen to convey precise shades of meaning. Bierce's style is stark and stripped, without excess verbiage but freighted with vast implications. Since it usually operates at more than one level, it poses a continual challenge and may trap the unwary. By its very nature, it forces the reader to think for himself.

The tendency toward compression and concision that found expression in the short story, moreover, Bierce developed even further in forms still briefer: the fable, the epigram, and the satirical definition. The wisdom that he had slowly and painfully acquired during a tumultuous life he learned to distill in sharp, pregnant observations, nearly always nonconformist and hence nearly always unpopular. He could condense a complicated philosophic, political, or social position to a short, pithy statement. Many of these are eminently quotable and still enjoy wide currency, like his definition of a prejudice as "A vagrant opinion without visible means of support."

Recent years have brought increasing attention to Bierce's writings, and an examination of his work affords a basis for understanding its continuing fascination, both here and abroad. The chapters that follow (8 to 11) present analyses of a number of his stories, together with a critical framework which enables the reader to interpret the tales more adequately than has yet been done. These analyses are followed (Chapter 12) by a discussion of the forms even more compressed than the short story. Finally, Chapter 13 presents a considered judgment of Bierce's significance today.

CHAPTER 8

Didactic Tales

ANYONE who has much familiarity with the stories of Ambrose Bierce knows that they make enormous demands on the reader. Uniformly short, they are written in an austere, terse style in which every word counts and in which large inferences must frequently be drawn from short passages—often single sentences or even, in some cases, single words. Because of the density and complexity of his stories, a representative group is examined in detail in four chapters, each devoted to a different genus: didactic tales, mimetic tales of passion, mimetic tales of moral choice, and mimetic tales of action.

Of Bierce's didactic tales, the three selected for close scrutiny are "Haïta the Shepherd," "Parker Adderson, Philosopher," and "The Famous Gilson Bequest." By an adaptation and modification of criteria developed by R. S. Crane for distinguishing a certain kind of poetry, didactic tales may be defined as "emotionalized arguments," in which the details of plot, character, and setting are "simply devices for enforcing the unifying dialectic." Such tales can best be approached through an examination of their thought, style, and arrangement of parts, since these stories are argumentative means for persuading the reader of their particular theses[1] —theses which Bierce frequently presented in other forms.

The three stories chosen for analysis are examples of three differing modes of dialectic. The first, "Haïta the Shepherd," is an example of three-term dialectic: each of the two chief characters presents a part of the truth, but the whole transcends and synthesizes both of the parts. The second, "Parker Adderson, Philosopher," exemplifies two-term dialectic: one character is used to present a false attitude which, through contrast, heightens the rhetorical effectiveness of the true attitude represented by the other character. The third story, "The Famous Gilson Bequest," presents an array of characters all of whom have the wrong attitude, which is condemned by the narrator both through explicit statements and through the use of puns, either verbal or represented dramatically by being incorporated into the action.

I *"Haïta the Shepherd"*

"Haïta the Shepherd"[2] is a didactic tale about the pursuit of happiness—a radiant blessing which comes to those who are truthful and do their duty, but who do not worship it *per se*. The thesis is similar to the one in Carlyle's *Sartor Resartus*. Commentaries are also furnished by a Bierce Epigram—"Happiness is lost by criticising it; sorrow by accepting it"[3] —and by one of his *Fantastic Fables*,[4] quoted below:

> Having been told by an angel that Noureddin Becar was the happiest man in the world, the Sultan caused him to be brought to the palace and said:
> "Impart to me, I command thee, the secret of thy happiness."
> "O father of the sun and the moon," answered Noureddin Becar, "I did not know that I was happy."
> "That," said the Sultan, "is the secret that I sought."
> Noureddin Becar retired in deep dejection, fearing that his new-found happiness might forsake him.

From many statements in Bierce's letters, we know that happiness for him was the greatest good in life.[5] "Haïta the Shepherd" has been commonly misread because it is assumed that the holy hermit speaks for Bierce. As a matter of fact, the story is a dialectical representation of two points of view: that of innocent and naive youth and that of cynical old age. But the narrator of the story emphasizes the fact that neither attitude is sound: "in the heart of Haïta the illusions of youth had not been supplanted by those of age and experience." The truth transcends what is perceived by both. This thesis is also presented in two more Bierce Epigrams: "Happiness has not to all the same name: to Youth she is known as the Future; Age knows her as the

Dream." "Experience is a revelation in the light of which
we renounce the errors of youth for those of age."[6]

The plot is the progression of Haïta from his youth,
when "his thoughts were pure and pleasant, for his life was
simple and his soul devoid of ambition," to the illusions of
age and experience, represented by the holy hermit. The
hermit does not tell Haïta that he can give him the truth;
he says, rather, "that age may minister to the hurts of
youth with such balms as it hath of its wisdom." When he
tells Haïta, at the end of the story, that happiness is "capricious for she imposeth conditions that man can not fulfill,
and delinquency is punished by desertion," and that, but
for Haïta's "indiscretion," he might have had happiness for
two moments rather than one, the hermit is not presenting
the didactic thesis of the story but "the illusions . . . of age
and experience." This interpretation is underlined by the
last sentence of the story; the only "wisdom" age has
brought him is cynicism, and the only "balms" he can offer
Haïta are half-truths.

Haïta himself never arrives at true wisdom concerning
happiness, yet he is used as a dialectical device for pointing
in its direction. He progresses through two stages. At the
beginning of the story, he is unthinkingly truthful and dutiful; therefore he catches "accidental glimpses of the minor
sylvan deities." But this kind of "happiness" is not appropriate to men, for what distinguishes them from animals is
the power of thought. Hence Haïta *must* think, for he is
human; otherwise, he would "turn into one of his own
sheep." What causes his beginning to think is pondering
about death, for which he has no name, but whose existence he infers from what happens to his sheep: "that horrible change to silence and decay."

One of Bierce's most firmly held convictions (reiterated
again and again) was that "to feel rightly one must think
and know rightly."[7] The emphasis on *right* thinking is very
important; man must not only think, he must think *rightly*
in order to feel rightly. Again, one may turn to the Epigrams (*Works*, VIII, 352, 362) for elucidation: "Thought
and emotion dwell apart. When the heart goes into the
head there is no dissension; only an eviction." "Train the
head, and the heart will take care of itself; a rascal is one
who knows not how to think."

Thus, when Haïta arrives at "the solemn inference that happiness may come if not sought, but if looked for will never be seen," he has arrived at only part of the truth, the first step in his march toward wisdom. For he grows abstracted and neglects his duty; his sheep either stray or grow "lean and ill." He therefore enters the second stage, but he enters it unthinkingly. He decides not to pursue unanswerable abstractions—"knowledge which the gods withhold"—but to do his duty as best he can. Then happiness comes, visiting him three times. But he has merely stumbled across the conditions which he must fulfill; since his awareness is not based on thinking rightly, happiness will not stay with him, for he cannot follow her instructions.

She tells him, first, that she must not be worshiped, because she is not a goddess; second, that she comes to those who are "truthful and dutiful." But Haïta *does* worship her, gazing at her "with reverence and rapture" and praying to her; and, of course, she disappears. When Haïta then does his duty by taking care of his flock, she comes back the next morning. But he disobeys her injunctions a second time by imploring her never again to leave him (he prays to her) and by wanting to "wrestle" and "run races" with her. But one cannot play games with happiness, and so she again disappears, not to return until Haïta once more does his duty, not by taking care of his sheep but by tending the feeble old hermit. She then reappears for the third and last time to find out if he has "learned wisdom." But he has not; he has been able to progress only part way, for he is not thinking rightly. Therefore, instead of analyzing and heeding her injunctions, he unwittingly repeats his disobedience; he asks her "to accept all the devotion" of his "heart and soul—after Hastur be served." Again, he is worshiping her instead of doing his duty; and she again disappears, never to return. Haïta, therefore, instead of being happy, is left with only the cold comforts of the hermit's cynicism.

A careful consideration of the didactic thesis of this story reveals not that continued happiness is unattainable, as the holy hermit believes, but something far more complex. The mindless contentment felt by Haïta during the first part of the story is not happiness; his is merely the innocent pleasure of animals. The first condition for human happiness is that it must be attained through thought. But the thinking has to be both accurate and complete. Man must realize that it is not enough to be truthful and dutiful; he must also attain the more difficult negative condition of not worshiping happiness. If he is able not only to arrive at a reasoned awareness of these arduous conditions (to think rightly) but also to act on the principles to which his thinking has led him, he will then be able to feel rightly: to realize such happiness that it will irradiate his life. Haïta himself never arrives at this stage; what he does approach is the cynicism of the holy hermit. But even this progress is better than the mindless contentment of his youth. The reader, however, through Haïta's failure, can learn where the young shepherd has gone wrong.

II *"Parker Adderson, Philosopher"*

"Parker Adderson, Philosopher,"[8] a didactic tale on the meaning and the acceptance of death, is closely related to "Haïta the Shepherd." Just as Haïta begins to grope toward the meaning of happiness by pondering on death, so General Clavering begins to grope toward the meaning of death by pondering on happiness. The man who can face death with courage is the one who knows and understands it, yet loves life. Flippancy and pseudo-philosophical rationalizations are defense mechanisms which crumble before the reality. These two points of view are represented dialectically by General Clavering and Parker Adderson; the title of the story is, of course, ironic. Indeed, the irony of the narrator throughout is admirably suited to the ironic way in which each of the two main characters is used to embody the attitude opposite to the one he thinks he is espousing.

General Clavering, "a Confederate officer of high rank and wide renown," is a "man of death" who was familiar with it even before his military career began. His bowie-knife is "a souvenir of the peaceful days when he was a civilian"—like the title, an ironic allusion. Parker Adderson is a spy who is unable to "think rightly"; he replaces reason with rationalization. And his failure to comprehend his own character is so complete that he believes he is capable of facing death with a jest. Instead of merely answering questions with his name and rank—as a spy was supposed to do—he seizes every opportunity for a flippant answer, thereby not only condemning himself but revealing valuable military information. He misunderstands his situation from the beginning, making false assumptions about the time and manner of his execution. When asked his name, he says he is "to lose it at daylight to-morrow morning," showing not only his pertness, but the rigidity of his thinking. He assumes that since, conventionally, spies were hanged at daybreak, his death will follow this pattern. What he does not realize is the implication for himself of the fact that "in General Clavering's command Confederate simplicity and penury of 'pomp and circumstance' had attained their highest development." The general, consequently, is not going to follow protocol with an elaborate execution at dawn; he will simply have Adderson taken out and shot when his guilt has been established by confession.

Clavering gives several hints that his prisoner is wrong; but the spy, who is consistently represented as a shallow thinker, does not pick them up. "How do you know that you are to die to-morrow morning?" he is asked. When he also gives a flippant answer to this question, General Clavering smiles. But his is a bone-chilling smile, as the narrator indicates: "No one in his power and out of his favor would have drawn any happy augury from that outward and visible sign of approval. It was neither genial nor infectious." The reader then learns that the dialogue has been, in effect, "a trial for a capital offense."

Adderson, however, continues his inappropriate punning, telling Clavering that the "disposition" of the Confederate troops is "morose." At this point "the general brightened again"; he now knows that the spy has not found out anything important about the military disposition of the Confederates. Having picked Adderson's brains, Clavering is ready to have him executed and writes the order. As the rain beats on the tent with a "dull, drum-like sound"—the only death march the spy is to have—the note ordering Adderson's execution is taken to the adjutant-general by Tassman, leaving the general and his prisoner alone together.

Having completed his military duties and prepared to dispose of Adderson as a spy, Clavering now turns his "hand-

some face" to him, regards him "not unkindly," and tries
to find out what he is like as a person, remarking, in a grim
double entendre: "It is a bad night, my man." Adderson,
thinking he is being clever, says: "For me, yes." He guesses
that the memorandum has to do with his execution, but he
continues to misinterpret the time and manner of it. Again,
however, the misinterpretation is his own. Clavering has
said merely that the note was "an order to be read to the
troops at *reveille* concerning your execution. [But he does
not say Adderson will *die* at reveille.] Also some notes for
the guidance of the provost-marshal in arranging the details
of that event." These two sentences mean one thing to the
general and quite another to Adderson, who quips that his
death will be "a spectacle"—which it will not be according
to the "Confederate simplicity" of Clavering's order. When
Clavering tries to make Adderson become serious by asking
if he wants to see a chaplain and when the prisoner answers
with another joke, the general, to whom dying *is* "a serious
matter," loses patience: "Good God, man! do you mean to
go to your death with nothing but jokes upon your lips?"

Adderson at this point drops his flippancy and embarks
on his second line of psychological defense, rationalizations,
which Clavering mulls over: "the man interested, perhaps
amused him—a type not previously encountered." But he is
unimpressed, for he knows that death cannot be rational-
ized away: it is "at least a loss—a loss of such happiness as
we have, and of opportunities for more." Adderson res-
ponds with another rationalization, which again Clavering
answers: "If the being dead is not a regrettable condition,
yet the becoming so—the act of dying—appears to be distinctly disagreeable to one who has not lost the power to
feel." This *power to feel*, as noted above, was very important in Bierce's psychological theory; it should be based
upon reason, but it must exist. As the reader later sees,
when Clavering himself is dying, his mind begins to wander;
a concomitant of this wandering is that he loses the power
to feel rightly, which, for Bierce, was based on being able
to think rightly. Consequently, nature has so arranged matters that, however the act of dying *appears* to the living, in
actual fact it can be faced with equanimity by the man
who understands death and loves life.

When Adderson answers Clavering by reverting to his jokes, the general loses interest in attempting to carry on a serious discussion with the spy; instead, he concentrates on his own thoughts, paying very little attention to Adderson, who continues in his misapprehension: "When I am hanged to-morrow morning . . . ." General Clavering merely looks impassively at him and exclaims almost inaudibly: "Death is horrible!" Since the general has seen many men die, the reader may surmise that at this point he is visualizing their corpses; and, as Bierce from his own experience made abundantly clear in articles and stories, death *is* horrible—to the living.[9]

But Clavering's thinking, at this stage, is only partially true; for he is considering death from the point of view of the living, not the dying. Nevertheless, he is reasoning, not rationalizing. When Adderson answers, first with another rationalization, then with a joke ("you cannot condemn me to heaven"), Clavering continues to ignore him; his thoughts turn to "an unfamiliar channel, but there they pursued their will independently to conclusions of their own." Finally the general announces that he himself should not like to die—"not to-night," another hint that Adderson fails to pick up. Clavering loves life, but, as is shortly revealed, he can accept death, in whose presence, as Bierce remarked elsewhere, "reason and philosophy are silent."[10]

Then Captain Hasterlick, the provost-marshal, enters; and Clavering orders him to take Adderson out to be executed. Symbolically, the storm is over and the moon is shining. But the peace of death really means nothing to Adderson, whose precarious defenses collapse at this point. He breaks down, becomes "frantic," and acts "with the fury of a madman." In the ensuing melee, he kills Hasterlick, who has mortally wounded General Clavering. "The spy had suffered the least damage," except mentally. He acts so strange everyone but the surgeon thinks he has gone crazy; the surgeon says he is "not insane . . . ; he is suffering from fright." When Clavering regains consciousness and orders Adderson shot, the reader learns that this order was part of the original memo and not an afterthought. As the order is executed, a volley rings out "upon the keen air of the midnight," but the dying general looks "pleasantly" at his

men and says "How silent it all is!" His mind wanders now,
a point underscored by the significant look that passes between surgeon and adjutant-general. The dying Clavering's
face is "suffused with a smile of ineffable sweetness." He
knows what is happening: "I suppose this must be death."
The thesis of "Parker Adderson, Philosopher," then, as
revealed by the dialectical interplay of ideas between the
spy and General Clavering, is that, however horrible death
may be to the living, it can be faced with serenity by the
man who understands life—and his own life in particular. A
capsule version of this argument is presented in the following Epigram (*Works*, VIII, 360):

> "Halt!—who goes there?"
> "Death."
> "Advance, Death, and give the countersign."
> "How needless! I care not to enter thy camp to-night. Thou
> shalt enter mine."
> "What! I a deserter?"
> "Nay, a great soldier. Thou shalt overcome all the enemies of
> mankind."
> "Who are they?"
> "Life and the Fear of Death."

In a letter to Danziger,[11] Bierce once wrote: "As to
death, there's nothing in it either to seek or to fear. It is
no more than life and a good deal easier to maintain. One
cannot die while alive and when dead one will not know;
so where's the hardship?" Although this statement sounds a
good deal like one of Adderson's rationalizations, it is explicitly the attitude dramatized by General Clavering. On
Adderson's lips, however, it is mere words—a mouthing of a
concept he cannot understand. He lives by conventions
(spies are always hanged at dawn), and his platitudes about
death are simply another convention which has no real
meaning for him since he does not understand life. Accordingly, he cannot accept death as part of its normal routine,
or as the necessary consequence, under military law, of
having been captured and convicted as a spy. When he
learns that the convention as to the time and manner of his
execution will not be followed, his merely conventional attitude toward death also breaks down.

III *"The Famous Gilson Bequest"*

The third didactic tale not only anticipates Mark Twain's "The Man That Corrupted Hadleyburg" (which was not written until 1899, and published in 1900) but also contains elements relating it to Dickens' *Bleak House* (which Bierce had read) and to Faulkner's *Requiem for a Nun.* Bierce's story, "The Famous Gilson Bequest,"[12] presents, like Twain's, the thesis that avarice can easily be aroused in man's soul, and that, when it becomes his ruling passion, it destroys his health, character, and mind; when it permeates his society, it tears to pieces the fabric of organized living. The disenchantment with "the damned human race" cuts even deeper in Bierce's story than in Twain's, however. Greed is a marked component of man's makeup in both stories, but Bierce goes beyond this recognition: such elements of righteousness as do exist in the avaricious soul emerge only when sanity is lost.

The narrator makes an artful use of puns in presenting and universalizing his thesis; when gold is discovered at "Mammon Hill," the mining town where most of the action takes place, it draws the entire population of "New Jerusalem," a nearby camp. The leading gambling establishment of Mammon Hill is called a "bank." And, at the conclusion of the story, the coffins in the cemetery become "sluice boxes" when they are flooded by the swollen Cat Creek after a season of rains; Gilson's guilt (about which there has been some doubt as the story progressed) is made clear through the actions of his ghost, which is represented as "cleaning up the dust" of his neighbors' mortal remains and as adding it to his own coffin, just as Gilson was accused of robbing gold dust from his neighbors' sluice boxes.

Even at its best, the mining camp is inhabited by a sorry lot of citizens, who left New Jerusalem drawn solely by the lure of mammon. Hangings are so common that their site is called simply "The Tree," and they are little better than lynchings, for, once society has "rendered its verdict," a trial is only a "decent formality" whose speed and meaninglessness are emphasized when Gilson is "tried, convicted, ... sentenced" to be "strung up," and hanged—all in one morning, less than twenty-four hours after his arrest.

Although the "society" that dispenses this drumhead justice has a "respectable" as well as an "opposite, or

rather . . . opposing, element," the division rests merely on
the saloon that each frequents. The "stern local code of
morality" sanctions draw poker and faro as honest means
of earning a living, and calling road-agency "highway robbery" is regarded as rather "harsh." Mammon Hill's "most
honored citizen" is the saloon proprietor, Jo. Bentley, who
welcomes Gilson's gambling business, even though it appears that Gilson, who has no visible means of support and
who loses more money than he has ever won, must be a
robber. Eventually, however, because of Henry Brentshaw's
idée fixe that Gilson was a thief, and his frequent declara-
tions of this belief, Bentley, "at a considerable personal
sacrifice," but "fearing . . . to lose the more profitable patronage" of Brentshaw, intimates that only those "of notorious commercial righteousness and social good repute"
may have "the privilege of losing money" at "this bank."

When it seems apparent that society has condemned
Gilson, he shows "signs of an altered life if not a changed
heart." The narrator is careful not to state in so many
words either that Gilson had been a thief or that he had
reformed. The reader could infer from the ambiguous account, however, that Gilson had merely turned from stealing gold dust to highway robbery and horse rustling. But
such an assumption on the reader's part rests on circumstantial evidence that is no more conclusive than that on
which Mammon Hill convicted Gilson.

In any case, Henry Brentshaw discovers Gilson one night
in compromising circumstances seeming to indicate that he
is stealing Mr. Harper's bay mare; his arrest, trial, conviction, sentence, and hanging follow in short order. He re-
venges himself posthumously on Mammon Hill by playing a
trick similar to that of the mysterious stranger's on Hadleyburg. He leaves everything he possesses to Brentshaw
(mammon's cleverest representative), on condition that
Brentshaw bury his body. When this is done, a codicil to
his will is discovered which stipulates that anyone who can
prove in a law court during the next five years that he had
robbed sluice boxes is to be his heir. If his guilt cannot be
legally proved, his entire estate (minus court expenses) is to
go, however, to Brentshaw.

Such a will, which appears to have been written by a
pauper, is of merely academic interest and is treated as an

amusing joke by the followers of mammon. However, in order to go along with the gag, "a facetious legislature" hastily passes a law which enables the will to be executed. Thus the machinery of legal justice and government—corrupt from the start, as is later discovered—are born in Mammon Hill, as related in a passage unrivaled until William Faulkner, in *Requiem for a Nun*, described the origin of the courthouse in Yoknapatawpha County.

But it is soon discovered that Milton Gilson had, in fact, been a very rich man in the East. Immediately Mammon Hill is thrown into a "fever of excitement," as the battle rages between those who would like to establish his guilt legally—in an ex post facto trial conducted after he had already been executed—and Brentshaw, his chief accuser, who now reverses his position and is determined to establish Gilson's innocence. The trial is a frontier version of the Chancery suit in *Bleak House*. "For five long years the Territorial courts were occupied with litigation growing out of the Gilson bequest." Corruption, bribery, and perjury are the tools of both sides. The battle is not confined to the courts; it rages in "the press, the pulpit, the drawing-room," "the mart, the exchange, the school; in the gulches, and on the street corners." And, when the five years are at last ended, "the sun went down upon a region in which the moral sense was dead, the social conscience callous, the intellectual capacity dwarfed, enfeebled, and confused!"

Brentshaw has won, but at fearful expense. The least costly element has been the financial drain; he has squandered Gilson's entire estate in legally establishing, through paid witnesses, bribed judges, and expensive lawyers, Gilson's innocence. In the process, he has ruined himself physically, emotionally, and intellectually. The one settled notion that remains in his shattered mind is a reversal of his original *idée fixe*. Now convinced that Gilson was innocent, he is tortured by remorse for having hounded him to death; for Harper had testified (for a price) that Gilson was taking the horse with Harper's permission. Brentshaw's mind is too weakened to perceive anything anomalous in the fact that Gilson had paid with his life for not communicating this information at the time of his capture. He has also forgotten that Harper's testimony was purchased. The only idea his "wrecked intellect" can retain, which he holds

as "a sort of religious faith," "the one great central and
basic truth of life—the sole serene verity in a world of lies,"
is the conviction of Gilson's innocence. "All that Mr. Brentshaw had since done for the dead man's memory seemed
pitifully inadequate—most mean, paltry, and debased with
selfishness!"

At this point in the story, an astonishing peripety occurs
without which the didactic message would have been incomplete. For if the theme is man's susceptibility to avarice, then even Gilson himself, who appears to have been
the victim of injustice, must have been as greedy as his
persecutors. And the reader now learns that, despite his
riches, he was little better than a kleptomaniac. A harrowing last scene in the cemetery where heavy rains and a
flooded creek have exhumed the coffins, among which the
water gurgles "with low sobbings and stilly whispers," reveals the ghost of Milton Gilson, busily robbing the other
open coffins of their dust and adding it to his own, faithfully imitating all the movements of a miner washing gold
dust in his pan. Although it is immaterial whether the ghost
is "a phantasm of [Brentshaw's] disordered mind" or "a
solemn farce enacted by pranking existences" that have a
shadowy borderland reality, Bierce's transferral of "The
Famous Gilson Bequest" from *Can Such Things Be?* to *In
the Midst of Life* for the *Collected Works* indicates that he
himself favored the first interpretation. In any event, this
second violent reversal of Brentshaw's most cherished conviction is too much for the broken man, and he dies.

One must say, in conclusion, that Bierce's didactic tales
do not present a "moral" in any obvious sense such as that
championed by William Dean Howells. Indeed, the use of
literature for purposes of reform was anathema to Bierce.
As Berkove points out, "Bierce did not evangelize in the
sense of broadcast preaching, but in the sense of *convincing*
those of his readers intelligent enough to understand
him."[13] He presents, in his didactic tales, what Hawthorne
called "the truth of the human heart."[14]

CHAPTER 9

Mimetic Tales of Passion

DIFFERENT from didactic tales are mimetic tales, imitations of human experience so represented as to arouse in the reader a sequence of expectations and emotions. The kind of human experience imitated presents three broad categories of plots for mimetic tales: those concerned primarily with changes in thought and feeling on the part of the protagonist as a result of his situation; those concerned primarily with the development or degeneration of moral character because of an ethical choice the protagonist must make about what is for him a serious issue in life; and those which deal primarily with external actions performed by the protagonist in relation to his situation. The stories which utilize these three types of plots may be termed mimetic tales of passion, of moral choice, and of action. Furthermore, the ways in which any of these plots are represented to create different kinds of emotional effects on the reader give the various species of any genus of mimetic tale.[1]

Bierce's mimetic tales of passion all have in common protagonists who undergo changes in thought and feeling as reactions to the situations in which they find themselves. However, in order to grasp the particular impact of individual stories in this group, the species to which each belongs must be determined.

I *Tales of Ironical Terror*

Most of Bierce's mimetic tales of passion are those of ironical terror (including "An Occurrence at Owl Creek Bridge," "Chickamauga," "One of the Missing," "One Officer, One Man," and "The Man and the Snake").[2] In these stories, Bierce combined irony with terror in a specific way. In any terror tale, the emotional effect is basically an intense degree of fear. To this fear, Bierce adds, in these tales, an ironic twist, which rests primarily on a certain kind of relationship between plot and character, so that the reader feels an intense fear coupled with a bitter realization that it is cruelly inappropriate.

Fundamentally, this effect of ironical terror depends on a firm grasp of the connection among intellectual, emotional, and sensory factors in the human personality. In Bierce's tales of ironical terror, a character's reaction to given circumstances involves all three of these factors. First, he has an intellectual awareness of a dangerous situation—typically one which he believes threatens his life or his honor. Second, this knowledge arouses in him an emotion of fear, it deepens to terror, and frequently thence to madness. Third, this emotional involvement results in a particular kind of physical reaction—usually a tremendous heightening and acceleration of sensory perceptions, the latter often indicated by a slowing-up of subjective time.

Obviously the base of this psychology is the intellectual awareness of danger. Bierce, however, makes the intellectual awareness on which the whole psychology of his protagonist's terror rests a wrong one; hence all the emotional and sensory reactions which follow are erroneous, and the reader's perception of this gruesome inappropriateness to the real situation is what gives their peculiar distillation of horror to these tales.

Since the situation in terror stories must arouse fear, it must either be dangerous or be thought dangerous. Bierce's best tales of ironical terror can be divided into two groups: those in which the actual situation is harmful, with the protagonist conceiving it to be harmless and reacting accordingly; and those in which the actual situation is harmless, with the protagonist conceiving it to be harmful and reacting accordingly. In either of these groups, the reader may share the protagonist's misconception, not discovering the truth until the end of the story; or he may realize all along that the protagonist is wrong. What the reader's grasp of events will be is controlled by the narration.

In the first category are such stories as "An Occurrence at Owl Creek Bridge"[3] and "Chickamauga." In "Owl Creek Bridge," Peyton Farquhar, a captured guerrilla on the point of being hanged, undergoes sensations at first "unaccompanied by thought. The intellectual part of his nature was already effaced; he had power only to feel." Suddenly, however, "the power of thought was restored; he knew that the rope had broken and he had fallen into the stream . . . . His brain was as energetic as his arms and legs; he thought with the rapidity of lightning." He thinks (wrongly) that he has made a miraculous last-minute escape from being hanged. The lost child in "Chickamauga," whose mother has been killed and whose home has been destroyed in battle, believes that the group of maimed and bleeding soldiers he comes upon is "a merry spectacle," one reminding him "of the painted clown whom he had seen last summer in the circus." He fails to recognize his home when he sees its blazing ruins, and he also thinks them a pleasing sight.

Thus in both stories the protagonist thinks himself safe in what is really a harmful situation. Accompanying his intellectual misunderstanding are emotional reactions which are painfully *mal à propos.* Farquhar eagerly makes his way homeward (he thinks), joyfully anticipating a reunion with his wife. The boy in "Chickamauga" has a gay time playing with the pitiful specimens he comes upon, "heedless . . . of the dramatic contrast between his laughter and their own ghastly gravity." He even tries to ride pig-a-back on one of the crawling and broken soldiers, and he dances with glee about the flaming embers of his home.

In both stories the protagonist also has unusual physical reactions. Farquhar's senses are preternaturally acute: "Something in the awful disturbance of his organic system had so exalted and refined them that they made record of things never before perceived." He feels each ripple of water on his face; he sees the veining of individual leaves in the forest on the river bank, the insects on them, and the prismatic colors of the dew in the grass. He even sees through the rifle sights the eye of the man on the bridge who is firing at him. And he hears "the humming of the gnats. . . ; the beating of the dragon-flies' wings, the strokes of the water-spiders' legs," the rush of a fish's body. Accompanying these perceptions is the slowing of time; the interval between his falling and suffocating is "ages," and the ticking of his watch is so strong and sharp it "hurt[s] his ear like the thrust of a knife."

The "Chickamauga" boy, on the other hand, has senses which are subnormally dull. He is a deaf-mute, which accounts for his sleeping through the battle: "all unheard by him were the roar of the musketry, the shock of the cannon." When he recognizes the torn and mangled body of his dead mother, and a belated understanding bursts upon him, he can express himself only by "a series of inarticulate and indescribable cries—something between the chattering of an ape and the gobbling of a turkey—a startling, soulless, unholy sound, the language of a devil."

In "An Occurrence at Owl Creek Bridge," the reader, unless he be extremely acute, does not realize the true state of affairs until the end of the story, although, as Lawrence Berkove points out in a perceptive analysis,[4] the narrator gives some clues which the reader can subsequently find. In "Chickamauga," the reader is constantly aware of the true situation and of the irony of the boy's reaction to it.

In the second group of stories—represented by "One of the Missing," "The Man and the Snake," and "One Officer, One Man"—the technique of ironic terror is reversed. A basically harmless (or at least, not very harmful) situation is misinterpreted as an extremely perilous one. The protagonist has not only all the emotional reactions which would be appropriate to terrible danger but also (as in the stories of the first group) unusual physical sensations; and the story concludes with his death.

Jerome Searing, a scout in "One of the Missing," recovers consciousness to find himself lying trapped in a wrecked shanty; he faces the muzzle of his own rifle, pointed directly at his forehead. Convinced that the gun is still loaded and set on a hair-trigger, as it was before he was knocked senseless, he believes that it will go off if he makes the slightest move.

In "One Officer, One Man," Captain Graffenreid, under fire for the first time in a minor engagement, not only misinterprets his situation but his own character. Thinking himself a courageous man, "his spirit was buoyant, his faculties were riotous. He was in a state of mental exaltation." But after the shooting starts, "his conception of war" undergoes "a profound change. . . . The fire of battle was not now burning very brightly in this warrior's soul. From inaction had come introspection. He sought rather to analyze his feelings than distinguish himself by courage and devotion. The result was profoundly disappointing." In his change from ignorance to knowledge of his own character,

he realizes his cowardice; but he still thinks he is in a
dangerous battle.

Harker Brayton in "The Man and the Snake" is the guest
of a distinguished herpetologist who keeps his collection of
serpents at home. One evening, when Brayton is sitting in
his room reading, he glimpses a snake under the bed. He
thinks the reptile is trying to hypnotize him with its male-
volent glare. At first he is "more keenly conscious of the
incongruous nature of the situation than affected by its
perils; it was revolting, but absurd." He thinks of calling
the servant, but it occurs to him "that the act might subject him to the suspicion of fear, which he certainly did
not feel." Then he considers the offensive qualities of the
snake: "These thoughts shaped themselves with greater or
less definition in Brayton's mind and begot action. The
process is what we call consideration and decision. It is
thus that we are wise and unwise." But, when he over-
estimates his own powers of emotional resistance, he makes
a fatal mistake: "I am not so great a coward as to fear to
seem to myself afraid."

In all these cases, the protagonist reacts emotionally to
what he thinks is a situation of extreme jeopardy. Jerome
Searing is a brave man; and, as he creeps forward on his
scouting expedition, his pulse is "as regular, his nerves . . .
as steady as if he were trying to trap a sparrow." When he
sees the rifle pointed at his head and remembers he has left
it cocked, he is "affected with a feeling of uneasiness. But
that was as far as possible from fear." Gradually, however,
he becomes conscious of a dull ache in his forehead; when
he opens his eyes, it goes away; when he closes them, it
comes back. He grows more and more terrified. As he
stares at the gun barrel, the pain in his forehead deepens;
he lapses into unconsciousness and delirium: "Jerome
Searing, the man of courage, the formidable enemy, the
strong, resolute warrior, was as pale as a ghost. His jaw was
fallen; his eyes protruded; he trembled in every fibre; a
cold sweat bathed his entire body; he screamed with fear.
He was not insane—he was terrified."

Captain Graffenreid, as he hears his men laughing at his
cowardice, burns with "a fever of shame" and "the whole
range of his sensibilities" is affected. "The strain upon his
nervous organization was insupportable." Agitation also

grips Brayton, though he is a reasonable man. The snake's
horrible power over his imagination increases his fear; and
he, too, finally screams with terror.

In these stories, as in those of the first group, the protagonists react with unusual physical sensations. Searing "had
not before observed how light and feathery" the tops of
the distant trees were, "nor how darkly blue the sky was,
even among their branches, where they somewhat paled it
with their green. ... He heard the singing of birds, the
strange metallic note of the meadow lark." Time slows,
space contracts, and he becomes nothing but a bundle of
sensations: "No thoughts of home, of wife and children, of
country, of glory. The whole record of memory was effaced. The world had passed away—not a vestige remained.
Here in this confusion of timbers and boards is the sole
universe. Here is immortality in time—each pain an ever-
lasting life. The throbs tick off eternities."

Captain Graffenreid, in his state of terror, grows "hot
and cold by turns," pants like a dog, and forgets to breathe
"until reminded by vertigo." Harker Brayton is also affected physically; when he means to retreat, he finds that
he is unaccountably walking slowly forward. "The secret of
human action is an open one: something contracts our
muscles. Does it matter if we give to the preparatory molecular changes the name of will?" His face takes on "an
ashy pallor," he drops his chair and groans: "He heard,
somewhere, the continuous throbbing of a great drum, with
desultory bursts of far music, inconceivably sweet, like the
tones of an aeolian harp. ... The music ceased; rather, it
became by insensible degrees the distant roll of a retreating
thunder-storm. A landscape, glittering with sun and rain,
stretched before him, arched with a vivid rainbow framing
in its giant curve a hundred visible cities." The landscape
seems to rise up and vanish; he has fallen on the floor. His
face white and bloody, his eyes strained wide, his mouth
dripping with flakes of froth, he wriggles toward the snake
in convulsive movements.

All three men die of their fright: Brayton and Searing,
from sheer panic; Graffenreid, a suicide because he can no
longer tolerate the disorganization of his nervous system.
But all their terror and pain were needless—Searing's rifle
had already been discharged; Graffenreid's battle was a

mere skirmish; Brayton's snake was only a stuffed one with shoe-button eyes. In these stories, as in "Chickamauga" and in "An Occurrence at Owl Creek Bridge," Bierce has given the terror tale an ironic turn of the screw.

II *"A Resumed Identity"—Tale of Pathos*

Three other mimetic tales of passion, each of which belongs to a different species, are examined in more detail: "A Resumed Identity" (a tale of pathos), "A Tough Tussle" (a tragic tale), and "The Death of Halpin Frayser" (a tale of uncanny dread). "A Resumed Identity"[5] is based on two incidents in Bierce's own life. As a young second lieutenant under Brigadier General William B. Hazen, he had participated in the battle of Stones River (sometimes called the Battle of Murfreesboro), Tennessee, on December 31, 1862. Many years later, accompanied by Percival Pollard in the summer of 1907, he toured his old Civil War battlefields in the vicinity of Chattanooga, nostalgically recalling the events of almost half a century earlier. Out of these two experiences came "A Resumed Identity," a mimetic pathetic tale of passion.

As is the case with many of Bierce's stories, the relation of the chronological incidents of the plot to their representation is rather complicated. Since in order to understand this relation, it is necessary to know what has actually happened, a chronological account of the incidents as they occurred will be presented first. The action begins when a twenty-three-year-old lieutenant on General Hazen's staff suffers a head wound in the battle of Stones River. He is rendered unconscious, and when he comes to, goes into a state of fugue. His amnesia lasts for many years—long enough for him to become an old man, easily tired, with a dull voice and wrinkled skin. But the reader has no knowledge of what has happened to the protagonist during the time that has elapsed while these physical changes were taking place.

For some reason—which the reader also does not know—the lieutenant has come back alone to the scene where he lost his memory. It is a moonlit summer night, just before dawn, and a light fog covers the ground. He is standing facing west "on a low hill overlooking a wide expanse of forest and field." Running north and south "a hundred

yards away was a straight road, showing white in the moonlight." The conditions are perfect for an optical illusion.
At this point the man's memory returns, and he looks
"curiously about him on all sides, as one who among familiar surroundings is unable to determine his exact place and
part in the scheme of things." Understandably, he is confused; also understandably, he orients himself by relating
the present moment to what—in his mind—was the moment
immediately preceding it, when he was in the midst of a
battle whose outcome he does not even know. Thus condi-
tioned, he sees what he expects to see: a line of soldiers,
"dim and gray in the haze." They appear on the road a
quarter of a mile to the south and move slowly north:
cavalry, infantry, and artillery. As "the interminable procession" passes from "the obscurity to south . . . into the
obscurity to north," what puzzles the observer is that it
moves "with never a sound of voice, nor hoof, nor wheel."
Why this unaccountable silence? He may be deaf; but,
when he speaks aloud, he can hear his own voice, although
it sounds strange to him, having lost its "*timbre* and reso-
nance." He then theorizes that he must be standing in an
"acoustic shadow," a military phenomenon he had noted,
in which nothing could be heard of the most thunderous
engagements from a certain direction.
   But soon something else bothers him. The silent figures
are gray—and they are moving in the direction of Nashville.
If they are Confederates—as they seem to be—then the
Union has lost the battle, and he is in danger of capture.
He turns away and strides toward the east; when he reaches
"the safer seclusion of a clump of cedars," he looks back,
but, to his astonishment, the entire column has disap-
peared: "the straight white road lay bare and desolate in
the moonlight!" He is inexpressibly puzzled; where can the
soldiers have gone? The reader may surmise that, with the
graying light, the mist has cleared and the old man can no
longer visualize what he thought he saw. Another thing that
strikes him is the peaceful appearance of the scene: the
fields are cultivated, smoke rises from farmhouse roofs, a
Negro is hitching a team of mules to his plow. The protagonist, remembering that he had been wounded in the head,
looks at his hand after passing it through his hair. But there
is no blood.

He therefore turns and walks west toward the road. There he meets a physician, Dr. Stilling Malson, of Murfreesboro, who is returning home after a night call. The ex-soldier, who is dressed in civilian clothes, salutes the doctor and asks if he is an enemy. After a brief conversation, Dr. Malson surmises that he is dealing with a case of fugue. He recalls what he has read "about lost identity and the effect of familiar scenes in restoring it," and he treats the man with courtesy and gentleness. But eventually he makes a mistake. When the soldier says "Not two hours ago I saw a column of troops moving northward on this road," the physician opposes him with the statement that he had met "no troops," and the old man turns angrily away. The physician, though rather amused, has been professionally civil and noncommittal, neither impolite nor unsympathetic; but he feels "half-penitent."

Then the distracted old fellow, with "a distinct feeling of fatigue" after very slight effort, sits on a rock and looks at his hand. It is "lean and withered." He feels his face; it is "seamed and furrowed; he could trace the lines with the tips of his fingers." These marks of physical decay seem very strange, and they are not to be accounted for by "a mere bullet-stroke and a brief unconsciousness." Then, groping, he arrives at the conclusion that he has "been a long time in hospital." He assumes the period of his stay must have been several months, a belief supported by his sudden recollection, on this summer day, that the battle was in December. Then he comes upon a time-worn monument erected by Hazen's Brigade in memory of its soldiers killed at Stones River. It is "brown with age, weather-worn at the angles, spotted with moss and lichen. Between the massive blocks were strips of grass the leverage of whose roots had pushed them apart." The man feels "faint and sick"; and, when he sees "the reflection of his face, as in a mirror," in a pool of water, he is overcome and dies.

The representation of the action is not, however, so straightforward as this account. The story is divided into three parts, each with a subtitle. The first, "The Review as a Form of Welcome," is told from the point of view of the old man on the site of a historic battle when he is reverting to his original personality. The familiar scene makes him "see" soldiers, although it is summer and the battle was in winter. But, still disoriented, he does not at first think of this disparity. All he notices is the strange stillness of the army's movements and the tranquility of the pastoral landscape which he remembers as a battlefield. The second section, "When You have Lost Your Life Consult a Physician," is told as if seen through Dr. Malson's eyes, and the reader is given various professional clues as noted by a sympathetic and medically sophisticated observer. The third section, "The Danger of Looking into a Pool of Water," again represents the action from the point of view of the old man, as more and more facts impress themselves on his awareness until the full truth finally bursts upon him and he dies from the shock.

The effect on the reader is pain at the contemplation of unfulfilled opportunities in the life of someone to whom he wishes no harm. The protagonist is a man who has lived two separate but incomplete lives. The pathos lies in the fact that he cannot join the two. In a sense, he was "killed" at the Battle of Stones River as a young lieutenant. In another sense, nearly all his adult life, with no memories of childhood or youth, has been built on sand. The disjunction between the two halves of his personality is underscored by the narrator in the last sentence, when he says that the protagonist, dying, "yielded up the life that had spanned another life." The reader feels pathos in reflecting on the lieutenant's two wasted lives, in neither one of which he has been able to fulfill himself as a human being living out his allotted time.

III   "A Tough Tussle"—Tragic Tale

The next story, "A Tough Tussle,"[6] was transferred by Bierce from *In the Midst of Life* to *Can Such Things Be?* for the *Collected Works*, indicating that he wished to emphasize its apparent relation to the supernatural. One should keep in mind, however, that Bierce defined GHOST in *The Devil's Dictionary* as "the outward and visible sign of an inward fear." In "A Tough Tussle," what seems supernatural to the protagonist is given a realistic explanation in terms of his own character.

Lieutenant Brainerd Byring is "a brave and efficient officer" whose *hamartia* derives from two elements in his character, one innate and one based on his comparative inexperience "in the business of killing his fellow-men." To his "unusually acute sensibilities" and "keen sense of the beautiful," dead bodies are a hideous affront; accordingly, he feels for them a "reasonless antipathy" which is "something more than the physical and spiritual repugnance common to us all." He is therefore a better man, in respect to bravery, than others; "for nobody knew his horror of that which he was ever ready to incur." Yet in one regard his active imagination makes him a good officer, for "in his small way [he] was something of a strategist; if Napoleon had planned as intelligently at Waterloo [as Byring has done with his few men on the night the action of the story takes place] he would have won that memorable battle."

Nevertheless, the protagonist's military inexperience is emphasized. The battles he has been in—Philippi, Rich Mountain, Carrick's Ford, and Greenbrier—were all minor engagements in the early days of the Civil War in which Bierce himself had participated. Byring was commissioned because his captain had been killed and because he had "borne himself with such gallantry as not to attract the attention of his superior officers." The combination of his hypersensitivity to death and his relative inexperience makes him peculiarly susceptible to the situation in which he finds himself. As the story develops, he is overwhelmed by thoughts and feelings which transform him from a good and brave officer to a man who goes insane from terror, first stabbing a maggoty corpse repeatedly and then killing himself. The action is merely a device for externalizing the changes that take place in his mental and emotional reactions, caused by a combination of external circumstances—a "monstrous . . . alliance . . . of night and solitude and silence and the dead" (cf. "The Suitable Surroundings")—and psychological causes. These latter, in turn, are of two kinds: not only a racial heritage from primordial times, but also his own special sensitivity to corpses. He is able to rationalize the first of these, but against the second he has no defense but an ill-timed levity which is powerless to control his irrational emotions; and they break through the weak barriers he has erected.

The progress of the tale is a gradual unfolding of the successive changes in Byring's thoughts and emotions. When he first sees the body, he thinks it may be still living.

"Instinctively he adjusted the clasp of his sword-belt and laid hold of his pistol—again he was in a world of war, by occupation an assassin." When he realizes the body is a corpse, his "sickness and disgust" cause him to forget "military prudence" and to light a cigar. In the ensuing blackness he is momentarily relieved because he can no longer see the figure. But, when it appears again, he begins talking to himself: "Damn the thing! . . . What does it want?" It appears soulless to him. He tries to protect himself from the encroaching flood of emotion within him by looking away and humming a tune, which he breaks off in the middle. His next feeling is annoyance; then "a vague, indefinable feeling that was new to him. It was not fear, but rather a sense of the supernatural." Here he begins the defense of intellectualization; he does not believe in the supernatural, so he tries to rationalize his feelings by what Jung has interpreted as the collective unconscious:

> "I have inherited it. . . . I suppose it will require a thousand ages—perhaps ten thousand—for humanity to outgrow this feeling. Where and when did it originate? Away back, probably, in what is called the cradle of the human race—the plains of Central Asia. What we inherit as a superstition our barbarous ancestors must have held as a reasonable conviction. Doubtless they believed themselves justified by facts whose nature we cannot even conjecture in thinking a dead body a malign thing endowed with some strange power of mischief, with perhaps a will and a purpose to exert it. Possibly they had some awful form of religion of which that was one of the chief doctrines, sedulously taught by their priesthood, as ours teach the immortality of the soul. As the Aryans moved slowly on, to and through the Caucasus passes, and spread over Europe, new conditions of life must have resulted in the formulation of new religions. The old belief in the malevolence of the dead body was lost from the creeds and even perished from tradition, but it left its heritage of terror, which is transmitted from generation to generation—is as much a part of us as are our blood and bones."

Up to a point his rationalization is successful; then his eye falls on the corpse. He notices all the physical details of the dead body, which impresses him as "horrible." He tries levity as a defense, again talking to himself: "Bah! . . . he was an actor—he knows how to be dead." Then Byring "resolutely" looks away and resumes his "philosophizing": "It may be that our Central Asian ancestors had not the custom of burial. In that case it is easy to understand their fear of the dead, who really were a menace and an evil. They bred pestilences. Children were taught to avoid the places where they lay, and to run away if by inadvertence they came near a corpse." Then comes a reaction which might have saved him: "I think, indeed, I'd better go away from this chap."

If he had been able to act on this impulse, the defense might have worked. But two other factors now contribute to his eventual downfall: military necessity ("he had told his men in front and the officer in the rear who was to relieve him that he could at any time be found at that spot") and pride ("if he abandoned his post he feared they would think he feared the corpse"). His fear of ridicule is, at this point, stronger than his fear of the corpse. So he seats himself again and "to prove his courage looked boldly at the body." But his is a classic example of overcompensation; for, if he had been really brave, he would not have had to prove his courage. Like Harker Brayton in "The Man and the Snake," Byring is undone by the fear of being fearful.

The corpse, which now exerts a strange and irresistible fascination, arouses in Byring a whole series of physical reactions: "His teeth were clenched and he was breathing hard." As he analyzes these symptoms, he consciously relaxes—another defense, which affords him momentary relief and he laughs. But his levity, which has got completely out of hand, frightens him terribly: "Heavens! what sound was that? what mindless devil was uttering an unholy glee in mockery of human merriment? He sprang to his feet and looked about him, not recognizing his own laugh." His physical sensations become extreme; his legs give way, his whole body is drenched in perspiration, he can not even cry out. Utterly helpless in the grip of his terror, he can no longer control his actions. At this point the narrator reaffirms that "Lieutenant Byring was a brave and intelligent man." But the combination of external circumstances and the racial memory are too much for his unique sensitivity; "courage was not made for so rough use as that."

It cannot be overemphasized that, for Bierce, it was

necessary to know rightly in order to feel rightly. The second presupposes the first, and Byring's knowledge is flawed: he does not grasp the limitations of his own character in such circumstances as he finds himself. He has carefully analyzed the racial heritage of the death-fear all men share. But this knowledge is a merely abstract one. What he has not allowed for are the special elements in his own character which make him peculiarly susceptible to this universal repugnance: his imagination (which, in other respects, heightens his effectiveness as an officer), his relative lack of front-line experience, his pride in his tactical arrangements, and the *hubris* that prevents him from acknowledging the extent of his fear until it is too late for him to cope with the terror which overwhelms him.

The next stage for Byring is hallucinations; he thinks the figure "had moved," then that it "was visibly moving!" He loses all control when a shot rings out from the picket line; "it broke the spell of that enchanted man; it slew the silence and the solitude, dispersed the hindering host from Central Asia and released his modern manhood. With a cry like that of some great bird pouncing upon its prey he sprang forward, hot-hearted for action!" But the damage to his soul had already been done; release comes too late. He acts, not as a normal man, but as an insane one, stabbing the corpse repeatedly and then committing suicide. The little battle, like all the other engagements Byring had been in, was merely "an affair of out-posts." But his "tough tussle" was with the enemy which lay within him, and it has conquered.

This tragic tale of passion has a plot that is controlled by the successive stages in Byring's thought and feelings. The story arouses pity because the protagonist is a brave, fine man and a good officer; he does not deserve his fate. It arouses fear because the reader shares the ancestral memory which finally undoes Byring. The reader might not react to it like Byring, but these atavistic passions exist in him, too; and, under special circumstances, they could also break down his defenses.

IV *"The Death of Halpin Frayser"—Tale of Uncanny Dread*

"The Death of Halpin Frayser,"[7] a mimetic tale of passion, belongs to the species of uncanny dread. Elsewhere

Bierce remarks that "when Death comes cloaked in mystery he is terrible indeed,"[8] a fact which helps to account for the peculiar impact of the tales in this group. "The Death of Halpin Frayser," one of the greatest of these stories, requires the utmost precision in its interpretation.

The tale seems to rely on the supernatural—specifically mental telepathy and zombies—to account for the protagonist's death. Bierce makes use of a hypothetical sage named Hali to present, in the following epigraph,[9] what purports to be a philosophical underpinning for the existence of ghosts and zombies:

> For by death is wrought greater change than hath been shown. Whereas in general the spirit that removed cometh back upon occasion, and is sometimes seen of those in the flesh (appearing in the form of the body it bore) yet it hath happened that the veritable body without the spirit hath walked. And it is attested of those encountering who have lived to speak thereon that a lich so raised up hath no natural affection, nor remembrance thereof, but only hate. Also, it is known that some spirits which in life were benign become by death evil altogether.

By placing this epigraph at the beginning of the story, Bierce conditions the reader to a supernatural explanation of the events which are narrated. And the manner of representation makes such an explanation plausible. The protagonist, Halpin Frayser, has been out hunting. Late in the afternoon the sky grows overcast, he gets lost, and lies down to sleep in what seems to be a forest. Suddenly he wakes up, says "Catherine Larue," a name that means nothing to him, then falls asleep again. This time he has a horrible dream in which he is walking along a highway when he comes to a road branching off it. He unhesitatingly turns into the road, for he is "impelled by some imperious necessity," although he is convinced that it leads to "something evil." He is surrounded by a wan and baleful light, and blood drips from the surrounding trees and glitters from a depression in his path. The strange terror he feels is augmented by an inexplicable guilt for some unnamable crime he vainly seeks to identify. His dread is further aggravated by the murmurings of mysterious creatures which surround him on all sides. Finally, in a desperate attempt to perform some action, he shouts. The echoes die away, and he determines to leave a record of his persecutions; dipping a twig in the pool of blood, he writes rapidly in his pocket notebook.

As he writes, he hears a soulless laugh. Then he feels a "strange sensation" slowly overpowering him: "a mysterious mental assurance of some overpowering presence—some supernatural malevolence different in kind from the invisible existences that swarmed about him, and superior to them in power." Terrified, he struggles desperately to finish his writing, but suddenly his hands fall to his sides; "powerless to move or cry out, he found himself staring into the sharply drawn face and blank, dead eyes of his own mother, standing white and silent in the garments of the grave!" Although he and his mother had been very close, this apparition "stirred no love nor longing in his heart." He tries to run from it, but cannot move; and he stares helplessly at "the lusterless orbs of the apparition, which he knew was not a soul without a body, but that most dreadful of all existences infesting that haunted wood—a body without a soul! In its blank stare was neither love, nor pity, nor intelligence—nothing to which to address an appeal for mercy."

Suddenly the creature leaps upon him and grips his throat. Although he resists fiercely, "what mortal can cope with a creature of his dream? The imagination creating the enemy is already vanquished; the combat's result is the combat's cause." He is borne backward, and dreams that he is dead—as, in fact, he shortly is, strangled to death. His body, the neck and face purple-black and the throat horribly bruised, is discovered the next day by a deputy sheriff and a detective who are seeking the murderer of a Mrs. Branscom. Near the corpse is his notebook, with a gloomy lyric describing his passage through the enchanted wood. He has been lying on the grave of Catherine Larue, the murdered woman, who, the reader learns, was his mother.

The reader, who has been led by the narrator, step by step, is prone at first to explain the uncanny dread with which the recital of these events fills him by assuming the supernatural. The epigraph by "Hali" indicates the existence of hate-filled zombies. The events which take place in the "forest" are represented only through Frayser's nightmare. There is the strange coincidence that he should have

waked up from a sound sleep, spoken his mother's name
without recognizing it (she had been widowed, remarried,
and murdered by her second husband since the last time
Halpin Frayser saw her, although he does not know any of
these facts), and then had a terrifying dream in which she
appeared, now dead, regarding him "with the mindless
malevolence of a wild brute" before she leaped upon him
and strangled him. Halpin Frayser, who is not a poet, has
left a poem, written in red, in the style of his maternal
great-grandfather, Myron Bayne. In this poem he mentions
the "gloom of an enchanted wood," the stagnant air, the
"witch-light." And during the last afternoon and night of
his life, spreading clouds, which are described by the narrator in great detail, had slowly crept down the mountains
and covered Napa Valley, as if "with an intelligent design
to be absorbed," with "an ever-extending canopy, opaque
and gray." This dismal fog continued to descend until it
reached St. Helena, from whence came the two manhunt-
ers, in a "morning light [that] was wan and ghastly, with
neither color nor fire." Finally, Halpin Frayser has fallen
asleep and has been killed on his mother's grave.

Even to put this interpretation together requires a careful
reading of the four sections of the story and a matching of
points which may at first seem unrelated. Many readers,
having gone no further, rest content. And it is true that
even at this level, "The Death of Halpin Frayser" is effec-
tive and compelling. Anyone who continues to examine the
tale carefully, however, begins to doubt whether the solu-
tion is quite so simple. And for him, when he eventually
begins to understand the story, the effect of uncanny dread
is nearly hair-raising. To begin with, a number of facts are
left unexplained by recourse to the supernatural. When
Halpin Frayser's body is discovered by Holker and Jaralson,
it bears all the marks of a man who has been physically
strangled, not one who has died of horror. There are evi-
dences of "a furious struggle" and, alongside Frayser's hips,
"the unmistakable impressions of human knees." As Holker
and Jaralson are discussing the mystery, they hear "a laugh
so unnatural, so unhuman, so devilish," that it fills them
"with a sense of dread unspeakable!" The narrator, who
does not explain this laugh, leaves the reader to draw his
own conclusions—and what they will be are determined by

his interpretation of the story, for it ends here.

But Holker and Jaralson have actually given all the clues the reader needs to understand the realistic external drama. After her first husband's death, Katy Frayser had gone to California "to look up some relatives"—her son, obviously. She did not find him, for he had been shanghaied, taken off to sea, and shipwrecked. Eventually she married a man named Larue (alias Branscom), who went mad and cut her throat. Unshaven and unkempt, he revisited her grave nightly. When he sees a stranger lying on her tomb, he throttles him in a maniacal rage. And, when this second victim of his murderous fury is discovered, Larue laughs in soulless, joyless glee.

Only the poem remains to be explained. In discussing Halpin Frayser's Nashville background in Section II, the narrator states that, although Halpin was generally regarded as a throwback to Myron Bayne, he had never actually written any poetry. "Still, there was no knowing when the dormant faculty might wake and smite the lyre." And, if it should, the lyre has already been strung and tuned; for Frayser loves literature and, with his mother, has pored over the poetry of his distinguished forebear. Consequently, he would be so steeped in Bayne's style that his first writing might well be imitative enough, given his enation with his famous ancestor, for Jaralson to assign it immediately to Myron Bayne. The influence of heredity was a significant factor in Bierce's thinking, as is indicated in one of his Epigrams (*Works*, VIII, 363): "A man is the sum of his ancestors; to reform him you must begin with a dead ape and work downward through a million graves. He is like the lower end of a suspended chain; you can sway him slightly to the right or the left, but remove your hand and he falls into line with the other links."

But how was the poem composed? That it was written in red, scrawled hastily and almost illegibly, and unfinished, are really all the reader knows about it. Halpin Frayser's dream of scribbling it does not necessarily indicate that it was actually written just before his murder, although this clue is the only one the narrator gives as to its composition. Actually, Frayser could have started his poem in red ink at home, been unable to finish it, and carried it about with him. True, the reader is told that Halpin "was a poet

only . . . in his dream." Still, the composition of one unfinished poem hardly entitles a man to be called a poet
(Bierce always claimed, despite the large amount of verse
he had written, that he himself was not a poet). More
far-fetched, but still possible, is the theory that Frayser did
write it in a state of somnambulism, using a twig and the
blood from dead birds he had shot that day and was carrying in his game bag.

In spite of all these signs that Frayser was actually murdered by his insane stepfather, the narrator has nevertheless
set up all sorts of clues which point to a supernatural—and
superficial—explanation. Yet these clues are red herrings
whose trail the reader must be careful not to follow. Bierce
once wrote that "love as it is cannot be portrayed in a
literature dominated and enthralled by the debasing tyran-
ny which 'sentences letters' in the name of the Young
Girl."[10] And he also wrote of the sexual "vices that plague
us and sins that beset."[11] For Halpin Frayser's terrible and
doomed struggle is not only against a murderous psycho-
path; it is also played out on the arena of his soul. In "A
Tough Tussle" and in "A Watcher by the Dead" Bierce
used the collective unconscious as an element of thought.
In "The Death of Halpin Frayser," the reader of today
turns to Freud rather than to Jung for help, since many of
the phenomena in this story can be explained only by
psychoanalytical theory (much of which Freud himself had
acquired from a study of great literature).

The key to this interpretation is found in an observation
that the narrator makes in Section II to explain the close
ties between Halpin Frayser and his mother: "In these two
romantic natures was manifest in a signal way that neglected phenomenon, the dominance of the sexual element
in all the relations of life, strengthening, softening, and
beautifying even those of consanguinity. The two were
nearly inseparable, and by strangers observing their manner
were not infrequently mistaken for lovers." This straightforward description by Bierce is today—following Freud—
called the Oedipus complex. It could hardly be more explicit; Halpin Frayser and his mother are in love, and Bierce
specifically mentions the sexual element in their feeling for
each other. He has also explained this feeling on grounds
any analyst would accept: Frayser, the youngest child, "not

over robust," had been neglected by his father and spoiled
by his mother. And he had, as a result, adored her.

She in turn had focused her filial feeling on her grandfather, "the late and great Myron Bayne," an admiration
she had cunningly concealed from everyone except her
youngest son, who all members of the family concede
closely resembles his great-grandfather, "pretty faithfully re-
produc[ing] most of the mental and moral characteristics
ascribed by history and family tradition to the famous Colonial bard." Myron Bayne had been a poet; although
Halpin has never written any verse, he was "addicted to
literature"; like his mother, he was also "a devout disciple"
of Bayne's poetry; and their "common guilt" in this respect
was "an added tie between them."

As Halpin matures, the bond deepens: "If in [his] youth
his mother had 'spoiled' him, he had assuredly done his
part toward being spoiled. As he grew to . . . manhood . . .
the attachment between him and his beautiful mother—
whom from early childhood he had called Katy—became
yearly stronger and more tender." And it had a strong sexual component that increased rapidly as he passed from
childhood to adolescence to young manhood; indeed, he
kisses and fondles his mother in her boudoir as if he were
her lover instead of her son.

But such an attachment runs counter to the strongest
and deepest taboo of almost every society man knows anything about: incest. And inevitably Halpin Frayser must
have been growing disturbed about the nature of his feeling
for the beautiful dark-haired mother whom he called by her
first name and whose lover strangers assumed he was. He
therefore attempts to run away from an intolerable situation. He plans a trip to California on some vague legal
business and, with a trepidation he tries to conceal, tells
Katy his decision. She immediately pleads to go with him.
But she also has been uneasy.

Freud himself was not more convinced of the profound
psychological insights to be discovered in dreams than was
Bierce,[12] and Katy Frayser has had, in the light of her
relationship with her son, an extremely significant one.
Some unconscious source of wisdom has told her, through
the vision of her revered grandfather, who appears as young
and handsome as Halpin himself, that she has destroyed her

son's identity and strangled him. Her fingers even pain her and feel stiff after she wakes up. She does not, however, have a psychoanalyst to interpret her dream; and she takes it to mean that she will go to California with Halpin. He, however, having more insight than his mother—and consequently more fear of the direction their relation is taking —understands her dream well enough. "He was to be garroted on his native heath," a fate "more simple and immediate, if less tragic, . . . than a visit to the Pacific Coast." In this symbolic garroting, or psychic death, he will be strangled by mother love.

And so he flees from his own passion, while his dim father asserts himself strongly enough on the domestic hearth to keep his wife from following her son. Halpin arrives in San Francisco, where he is shanghaied aboard a ship wrecked in the South Pacific; he does not return for six years. He settles near St. Helena, and writes home for news and remittances. While waiting for a reply, he goes hunting one day and shoots a bag of doves. He gets lost on the way home, winds up in a tree-grown graveyard which he does not recognize as such, and falls asleep on his mother's grave. Just before falling asleep, the reader must assume, he sees the name "Catherine Larue" on the headboard; but, "utterly bewildered" at being lost and "overcome with fatigue," he falls immediately into a dreamless sleep without even being consciously aware that he has seen the name. Then he wakes up, pronounces it aloud, and falls asleep once more.

But the utterance of "Catherine" (Larue, of course, the name of his mother's second husband, meant nothing to him), coupled with the fact that he is daily awaiting news from the home he has not seen for six years, has been enough to trigger the memory of his adored "Katy." The dream itself is very revealing when analyzed in the light of Freud's teachings. The little bypath Frayser has turned into from the main road represents the digression from normal masculine development he has taken in concentrating his libido on his mother, even though he knows that "it led to something evil." Yet he turns into it because he is "impelled by some imperious necessity"—that same libido whose pressure he cannot resist. As he travels along, he comes to "a shallow pool" into which he dips his hand—surely a vaginal symbol. The pool is filled with blood, an indication of the danger this course represents to him. Meanwhile, he feels a growing terror "which seemed not incompatible with the fulfillment of a natural expectation." And, most significant of all, he is wracked by an inexplicable and terrible guilt, as if he had committed some monstrous crime, which he tries to identify "by tracing life backward in memory." Finally, he puts his little twig into the pool of blood—the symbolism here is obvious to any reader of this psychoanalytic age—and, as he does so, "a strange sensation began slowly to take possession of his body and his mind," a reaction whose meaning is also obvious.

As he pushes the twig "with terrible rapidity," the "sharply drawn face and blank, dead eyes of his own mother" appear before him. While the two regard each other, the world seems to grow "gray with age and sin." Then his mother springs upon him. After a moment's stout resistance, he leaps forward and the two strain together, wrestling fiercely. As he is borne backward, he sees his mother's "dead and drawn face" only a hand's breadth above his own.

And then "Halpin Frayser dreamed that he was dead"—for it has been recognized since the time of Sophocles that the man who has engaged in the sexual relations with his own mother clearly symbolized by this dream must pay a terrible price. (The bachelor Harker Brayton in "The Man and the Snake" was doomed from the moment he believed the serpent was looking at him "with his dead mother's eyes.") Oedipus acted in ignorance; Halpin Frayser struggled against the pitiless force of his attraction—but both succumbed. And it is the recognition of Katy and Halpin Frayser's humanity that inspires the reader with uncanny dread. This tale is not of zombies and the supernatural, but one which concerns universal psychological forces just as mysterious as any spectral encounter and far more menacing.

The tales of mimetic passion discussed in this chapter, in which Bierce probes the depths of the human psyche, are among his greatest contributions to the short-story form. Their profound insight reveals his great understanding and deep compassion for the soul tortured by circumstances it can face only with the agonized courage of supreme suffering.

CHAPTER *10*

Mimetic Tales of Moral Choice

BIERCE'S mimetic tales of moral choice place their protagonists in situations where they must make crucial decisions involving a conflict between two value systems, both of which they adhere to. The specific emotional effect of such stories is determined by the character of the protagonist, the circumstances in which his choice is made, its consequences, and the manner of representation. In evaluating his tales of moral choice, one should keep in mind Bierce's belief that "the wisdom of an act is not to be determined by the outcome, but by the performer's reasonable expectation of success."[1] He expressed a similar idea in "A Lacking Factor," a short verse in *The Scrap Heap* (*Works*, IV, 360):

"You acted unwisely," I cried, "as you see
  By the outcome." He calmly eyed me:
"When choosing the course of my action," said he,
  "I had not the outcome to guide me."

In this chapter three of Bierce's mimetic tales of moral choice are analyzed, each exemplifying a different species: "The Affair at Coulter's Notch" (a tale of moral indignation), "A Son of the Gods" (a pathetic tale), and "A Horseman in the Sky" (a tragic tale).

I *"The Affair at Coulter's Notch"*—
Tale of Moral Indignation

"The Affair at Coulter's Notch"[2] creates its effect of moral indignation in part because of the disparity between the action and the representation of the plot, for only gradually are the reasons for the strange behavior of the leading characters—the general, the colonel, and Coulter himself—made clear. In the discussion which follows, the concentration is on the *action*—not on the representation—which began

115

when Coulter, a Southerner, threw in his lot with the Union.
The rest of his family—including his wife—remained loyal to
the Confederacy. After his departure for the front as an artillery officer, a thoroughly despicable Federal general, a division commander, was camped one summer for several weeks
in the neighborhood of Coulter's home. When he made ad-
vances to Coulter's wife, "a red-hot Secessionist, . . . but . . .
a good wife and high-bred lady," she repelled his unwelcome
attentions and complained to army headquarters, with the
result that he was transferred. Almost immediately he began
to plan a cowardly revenge on the woman who had spurned
him. His first step was to get Captain Coulter's battery assigned to his division. Coulter soon earned the admiration of
the colonel in charge of his brigade, who praised him warmly
to the general.

Eventually, the thwarted seducer's dark opportunity came,
and at this juncture the representation of the plot begins. The
general's division has driven the enemy back, but the Southern commander has left a rearguard of twelve guns on a ridge
facing the advancing Federal troops. Most of these guns were
visible from several points along a higher ridge on either side
of a notch in the crest of a hill that is held by the Federal
infantry, who are screened from fire. But the general, inexplicably to his senior officers, has ordered his infantrymen not
to pick off the Confederate guns. The one vulnerable point
on the Union side is the notch, traversed by a road; and, as
the Federal cavalry attempts to advance through this narrow
pass, its avant garde is slaughtered. The general and the colonel commanding Coulter's brigade make a quick reconnais-
sance of this exposed position, where three or four horses
and men have already died. From the notch all the Confederate guns but one are "masked by the trees of an or-
chard; that one . . . was on an open lawn directly in front of a
rather grandiose building"—Coulter's home.

The general then suggests that Coulter place a gun in this
pass. The colonel, who at first cannot believe his superior is
serious, answers: "There is room for only one gun, General—
one against twelve." The commander answers him "with
something like, yet not altogether like, a smile," indicating
ironically that the wonderful Coulter can bring up his guns,
one at a time, and fire them against the twelve ranged against
him. The colonel is angered, but he is bound by "the spirit of

military subordination" to carry out the order. When Captain Coulter comes riding up to the pass, he intently examines his surroundings. The colonel then tells him that the general has directed him to engage, with the single gun which is all the pass can hold at one time, the twelve Confederate pieces on the next ridge. This suicidal order is greeted by the young artillery officer with "a blank silence," while the stolid general looks away. Then Coulter asks if the guns are near the house; when the colonel, remarking that Coulter has "been over this road before," says they are "directly at the house," the pale-faced captain asks in a cracked voice if it is imperative the guns be engaged. The colonel, who has been commending Coulter's courage, is astonished and humiliated; but the general's "set, immobile face" remains "as hard as bronze."

Now Coulter has to make his agonized choice between disobeying orders or firing on his own home and family. What his feelings are the reader can infer only from his awkward behavior. Since the action also involves grave danger to himself and his men, it is easy, at this point in the representation, to suppose that his reluctance is due to cowardice—and this, indeed, is the assumption the colonel makes. The general's strange order and unfeeling reaction are attributed by the colonel to "a recent conversation between them [in which] Captain Coulter's courage had been too highly extolled." This inference gains weight from the fact that twice, in discussing the gunnery officer with the colonel, the general refers to him as "your brave Coulter." His apparent cowardice seemingly indicates that the colonel had misjudged his man, a belief that adds to the colonel's mortification.

But balanced on the opposite side of the scale from Coulter's love for his wife and child is his concept of military duty. He had already exercised one portentous option when he chose the Union over the Confederacy. It is unlikely that he could know of the general's attempted dalliance with his wife; consequently, the order, to him, undoubtedly seems like a tragic coincidence whose potentiality was implicit in his decision to put national interests above regional ones. And, at this fateful moment, he, and he alone, must decide how serious his commitment to the Union cause was.

And so, just as the colonel is about to order his arrest, the scale tips and Coulter makes his heart-breaking choice, which

may be a trifle eased by the probability of his own death as
he turns away to execute the general's order. He brings up his
first gun, which immediately begins firing. A "ghastly contest
. . . , without vicissitudes, its alternations only different degrees of despair," begins, in which four Union guns are dis-
abled and their gunners killed or wounded. The Federal
shells, aimed at the one Confederate gun "that maintained its
place in the open—the lawn in front of the house," explode
about this piece continually, some of them landing in the
dwelling. The colonel is torn between shame at Coulter's
"damned reluctance to obey orders" and controlled fury at
the general for "this uncommon way of amusing the rearguard of a retreating enemy" when the commander of the
Union infantry regiment sends for permission to silence the
Confederate guns. The colonel, who would like nothing better himself than such infantry action, is forced to tell the
messenger that "the general's orders for the infantry not to
fire are still in force."

At this point, the adjutant-general reports the gossip about
the general and Mrs. Coulter. With this story, the colonel
feels he can act; and he goes to direct Coulter's immediate
withdrawal. When he reaches the defile, he finds a smoking
hell, littered with dead and wounded, in which lie the wrecks
of four guns. A fifth piece is now firing, handled by "demons
of the pit!" Coulter himself is "a fiend seven times damned
. . . , with an unearthly regard, his teeth flashing between his
black lips, his eyes, fierce and expanded, burning like coals
beneath his bloody brow." As he obeys the command to
withdraw, the enemy ceases fire; and the pass is at last open
to the advancing Federal troops. An hour later the colonel
has established his headquarters in Coulter's house. During
supper, hearing strange noises in the basement, he descends
with a staff officer and an orderly. There they discover the
weeping Coulter with his dead wife and baby clutched in his
arms; the baby's foot has been blown away.

This scene is as far as the story takes the reader; his reaction is one of moral indignation that is directed and guided
by the normative standards of the colonel. Like him, the
reader was puzzled by Coulter's seeming cowardice; like him,
he was disturbed and angry at the general's meaningless orders which brought unnecessary injury and death to many
men. And, when the colonel got the key to the general's

strange behavior, the reader was relieved that he could at last act purposively.

But his action was too late. The damage had already been done to the one exposed gun in front of Coulter's house, and the Confederates had stopped firing at the very moment the colonel arrived to send Coulter to the rear. The reader may surmise that the general will face a court-martial, but his punishment will do the tortured husband and father no good; for he had already been forced, by a military hierarchy perverted to the basest possible use, to destroy his home and his own family. The reader is left only with a sense of moral indignation at the depraved character whose sadistic drive for revenge has brought about such terrible carnage.

II *"A Son of the Gods"*—Tale of Pathos

"A Son of the Gods: A Study in the Present Tense"[3] is a pathetic mimetic tale of moral choice. Its genesis probably lay in two actual incidents of Bierce's own experience during the Civil War. At the Battle of Shiloh, the Confederates were in force behind a small rise on the far side of an open field. Bierce, assuming (as did the other Federals) that they had retreated, led a platoon across the plain, expecting at most to be opposed by a line of skirmishers. The Southern forces lay low until the advancing soldiers were almost upon them, when they opened fire, causing fearful destruction. Bierce's men retreated as quickly as possible to the woods on the near side of the field, but the losses were dreadful. A Union colonel "had been a calm and apparently impartial spectator."[4]

Having, apparently, learned a grim lesson from this tragic episode, Bierce was determined to guard against its recurrence when a similar tactical situation arose during the Battle of Nashville. According to an account he later wrote, he told the Federal commander that it was unnecessary to "throw out any advance guard as a precaution against" ambuscade; Bierce himself would "act in that perilous capacity." Saying that he "never felt so brave" in his entire life, he "dashed forward through every open space into every suspicious looking wood and spurred to the crest of every hill, exposing [himself] recklessly to draw the Confederate fire and disclose their position."[5] His heroism turned out to be superfluous, however; the enemy had already withdrawn.

Nevertheless, keeping in mind Bierce's Epigram (*Works*,

VIII, 368)—"Courage is the acceptance of the gambler's chance: a brave man bets against the game of the gods"—it is easy to see how a selection of facts from both these autobiographical incidents could have resulted in a very different outcome. If, at Shiloh, a single officer *had* volunteered to draw the fire of Confederate troops who might be concealed in ambush, as Bierce had done at Nashville, what would have been the result? The imagined consequence was transmuted into high art in one of Bierce's finest stories, "A Son of the Gods." In the account of his Nashville sally, Bierce describes his own action in tones of levity, being careful not to paint himself a hero. But in the story, the same choice is treated with high seriousness; the narrator is cast as one of the onlookers; and the young officer becomes a "military Christ!"

As has been emphasized repeatedly, Bierce believed that, in order to feel rightly, one must first think rightly. Impulsive, irrational decisions lead to catastrophe. In "A Son of the Gods" this point is driven home as it is not in "The Affair at Coulter's Notch." In that story neither Captain Coulter nor the colonel has all the facts. Since their moral choices are made without complete knowledge, their thinking as such cannot be faulted. In "A Son of the Gods," however, the young officer, the corps commander, and the army itself all choose in full awareness of the circumstances.

The situation involves an advancing Federal army which has been halted in a forest by "a formidable obstacle"—a mile of open ground. Beyond it rises the crest of a hill, with a stone wall and hedge just behind it. Are the Confederates lying in ambush behind this shelter; and, if so, what are their numbers and disposition? If they have already withdrawn, then it is safe for the Union army to continue its advance. But, if they have not, any attacking soldiers would be exposed to murderous fire and a very different strategy would be necessary: the enemy would have to be maneuvered out by destroying his communication lines.

The problem, then, as everyone knows, is to acquire this vital information. The first moral choice is made by the heroic officer who decides to risk his life in order to save a line of exploring skirmishers from possible slaughter. Have the Confederates retreated or have they only retired to regroup their forces? The possibilities are not equally weighted. At the beginning of the story this paragraph occurs: "From the edge of the wood leading up the acclivity are the tracks of horses and wheels—the wheels of cannon. The yellow grass is beaten down by the feet of infantry. Clearly they have passed this way in thousands; they have not withdrawn by the country roads. This is significant—it is the difference between retiring and retreating." Consequently, there is some indication that the enemy has fled in defeat, and that the gallant officer, although he is taking a dangerous chance, will probably come through alive.

However, he cannot act without orders. And so he engages in a "brief colloquy" with his corps commander, who also must choose. He has to know the strength and deployment of the Confederate troops before proceeding farther. His position makes him responsible for all his men; is it better to risk one life or the lives of many? The choice is a painful one: "At what a dear rate an army must sometimes purchase knowledge! 'Let me pay all,' says this gallant man—this military Christ!" The commander is, understandably, at first indisposed to grant his young officer's request. Yet if, by doing so, he can save a large number of the lives entrusted to his care, he clearly must grant it. And he does, for the appeal is a sensible one: it is neither "an instance of bravado, nor, on the other hand, a needless sacrifice of self."

But now the soldiers also must make a moral choice. At first they had thought the dashing officer a "fool" who acted as if he were "on parade" as an "edition of the Poetry of War." Even as they laughed derisively, however, they noticed his careless, handsome grace. And, as they realize what he is doing, they find his courage infectious: "How glorious! Gods! what would we not give to be in his place—with his soul!" Significantly, they do not think of his *mind*, but of his *soul*, which draws their own souls after him. "But we remember that we laughed! . . . O, if he would but turn—if he could but see the love, the adoration, the atonement! . . . All are watching with suspended breath and beating hearts the outcome of an act involving the life of one man. Such is the magnetism of courage and devotion."

The young officer, on the other hand, continues to make his choices with his head. The only hope for his life is that the crest is clear. "It is necessary either that he return unharmed or be shot to death before our eyes. Only so shall we know how to act. If captured—why, that might have been done by a half-dozen stragglers." He gets a glimpse of the troops beyond the ridge, however, and knows immediately that he is doomed. He makes the best possible use of his few remaining moments by wheeling back and forth in order to get as many of the Confederates to shoot as possible. They, on their part, are straining to hold their fire. In this "extraordinary contest of intellect between a man and an army," the man wins. He seduces the enemy, all along their line of ambush, into firing at him, thereby revealing themselves. After his horse is shot from under him, he turns to his own men with uplifted saber and brings it down in a "hero's salute to death and history."

But the intellect of his own army is no firmer than that of the Confederates. Inspired by his courage and completely ignoring the very real tactical reason for it, they all run forward, "choking with emotion," against orders. "The rear battalions alone are in obedience." The front lines have made their moral choice, and they have made it on the basis, not of reason, but of feeling. Fortunately for the Union army, the commander is not swept away. He keeps his head, and saves the army from complete rout. Unmoving as "an equestrian statue," he stands steadfast with his "huddled escort" as the army flows around him "like tide waves parted by a rock. Not a sign of feeling in his face; he is thinking." He calmly addresses his bugler, who gives the signal; and the army sullenly withdraws. Some soldiers have been saved by the commander's coolness; nevertheless, the field is strewn with bodies. Ironically, much of the value of the young officer's gallantry has been wasted because the men whom his act could have saved allowed themselves to be ruled by their hearts instead of their heads. And the terrible pathos of this story lies in the fact that, as he dies, he knows how useless his own death was: "Ah, those many, many needless dead! That great soul whose beautiful body is lying over yonder . . . —could it not have been spared the bitter consciousness of a vain devotion?" Then comes an element of thought in this tale: "Would one exception have marred too much the pitiless perfection of the divine, eternal plan?"

This "divine, eternal plan" is clearly neither a Calvinistic nor a materialistic determinism; it is the nature of man. He *is* ruled by his heart rather than his head in most cases requiring a moral choice. Bierce in story after story attests to the power the emotions have and to the fact that reason cannot always control them. And, when it cannot, disaster results. The army knows fully as well as the commander what the purpose of the officer's daring is. But the soldiers, unlike their superior, make the wrong choice because their emotions overpower their reason.

This view is supported by the manner of representation: a combination of narrative and dramatic. The first paragraph begins dramatically, like stage directions, with incomplete sentences. The narrative part is in the present tense, as the subtitle indicates; it is written in the first person by a staff officer who observes the action, and who addresses the reader directly as "you." All these devices are very important elements in making the reader one with the emotional army; he sees the rational and detached commander from the outside, just as the army sees him. And he is left to face this question in his own soul: given a comparable crisis, would his action be based on thought or on emotion?

III   *"A Horseman in the Sky"—Tragic Tale*

"A Horseman in the Sky"[6] is a mimetic tragic tale of moral choice in which the setting is crucial. Having been a topographical officer in the Civil War, Bierce describes in Section I of the story, with the careful detail of an engineer, the physical conformation of an area in the Cheat River hills and valley, near Grafton, West Virginia, where he had himself served. A young Union soldier is a lookout on the crest of a ridge. North of it, from the point where he is stationed, a road leads down the hill to a valley where five regiments of Federal infantry are bivouacked. At his post, the road angles west along the summit of the ridge for a hundred yards, until it meets a large rock overlooking the Federal position. There it turns abruptly south down the opposite side of the ridge, at whose foot there is an encampment of Confederates.

The Federal soldiers, who plan to cross the ridge that night and to fall on the Confederates in a surprise attack, are in a particularly exposed location: a "military rat-trap, in which half a hundred men in possession of the exits might have starved an army to submission." Consequently, it is essential that the enemy not discover them; and for this reason a sentry has been posted on the ridge a hundred yards east of the outjutting rock.

The importance of the sentry's vigilance is emphasized in Section I. Dereliction on his part would place five Union regiments in mortal peril. But, stationed alone at this vital spot, he was "asleep at his post of duty," a capital offense in the military code. The seriousness of his transgression is made explicit by the narrator. Death, he asserts, is "the just and legal penalty" for the "crime" of this "unfaithful sentinel." In Section I, no details about him which would engage the reader's sympathy are presented; he is simply a criminal asleep on watch, whose lack of vigilance imperils all his fellows. If discovered, he would be executed—and rightly so.

Section II, however, reverts to the beginning of the action; and the reader learns something of the character and background of the lookout, Private Carter Druse. A young Virginian whose home was near Grafton, he knows the area; this is one reason for his present assignment. The only child of wealthy and cultivated parents, he had chosen to enlist in a Union regiment. His father, like Katy's husband in "The Death of Halpin Frayser," is "what no Southern man of means is not—a politician"; he is devoted not so much to his country as to "his section and State."

Consequently, the senior Druse reacted to the news that his son's sympathies were with the North after the manner of his Southern, Confederate class and region. A significant passage represents the confrontation:

> The father lifted his leonine head, looked at the son a moment in silence, and replied: "Well, go, sir, and whatever may occur do what you conceive to be your duty. Virginia, to which you are a traitor, must get on without you. Should we both live to the end of the war, we will speak further of the matter. Your mother, as the physician has informed you, is in a most critical condition; at the best she cannot be with us longer than a few weeks, but that time is precious. It would be better not to disturb her."
>
> So Carter Druse, bowing reverently to his father, who returned the salute with a stately courtesy that masked a breaking heart, left the home of his childhood to go soldiering.

One word in Druse's speech is apt to attract attention: why does the father call his son "sir"? This form of address, still common in the South, was very common at the time of the Civil War, but not in an intimate family situation where a respected elder was addressing a man a generation younger, particularly his own son. A little thought shows that Carter's father is reverting to the code *duello*, which could exist only between gentlemen and equals, and which followed rigid and formal rules of etiquette.[7] All that is implied in the elder Druse's "stately courtesy" is summarized when he addresses his son as "sir": Carter is a gentleman and an equal, but he is a "traitor" to Virginia who must be challenged. However, Mrs. Druse is dying and must not be disturbed. Even discussion of Carter's decision and the duel it will entail—provided the fortunes of war do not settle the issue—will have to be postponed. But, if her husband and son both live, they must eventually meet on the field of honor.

Nevertheless, the two Druses belong to different generations: Carter's sympathies are with the North, but he does not, in turn, think of the older man as a "traitor" to the Union. Because the son respects and loves his father, however, he does go through the motions of picking up the glove. Yet, as he bows "reverently," the reader may be sure that he is deciding, should the occasion arise, to fire into the air.

Carter becomes a courageous, conscientious soldier; but, like his fellows, he had marched all the previous day and night. Unlike them, he is still on duty, alone in a critical spot. On this sunny autumn afternoon, outraged nature takes her revenge; and he falls asleep. The reader may ask why such excessive demands are put upon him for thirty hours or more? At the least, why was a second soldier not assigned along with him? But the reader knows the answer from indications that Druse's commander is not overly solicitous for the welfare of his men. He is "foolish," he has bivouacked his soldiers in a "military rat-trap," and then he has permitted them to water their horses "in plain view from a dozen summits!"

The reader begins, therefore, to feel more and more sympathetic toward Carter Druse, despite his negligence. He is "brave, compassionate," and a man of taste: when, inexplicably, he wakes up and sees a Confederate horseman posed on the rock overlooking the valley, his first reaction is "a keen artistic delight." The silhouette looks like "a Grecian god carved in . . . marble," and the horse like "a cameo." He thinks of the figure as "a noble work of art"

commemorating a "heroic past of which he had been an inglorious part." He is already feeling guilty about having
fallen asleep at his post when he realizes the gray-clad
figure is his father.

He is confronted with a terrible choice. Must he kill his
parent, thereby saving his fellows? Or should he refrain
from shooting, dooming his comrades? His struggle is an
agonized one: "he shook in every limb, turned faint, and
saw the statuesque group before him as black figures, rising,
falling, moving unsteadily in arcs of circles in a fiery sky
. . . . This courageous gentleman and hardy soldier was near
swooning from intensity of emotion." But he makes his
choice: "mind, heart, and eyes were clear, conscience and
reason sound . . . . The duty of the soldier was plain." Just
before he fires, he remembers his father's last injunction.
The one concession he makes to filial feeling is to aim at
the horse, not its rider. Nevertheless, he is calm and tran-
quil as he fires; "duty had conquered; the spirit had said to
the body: 'Peace, be still.' "

But why is this devoted son able to make his terrible
choice with so much clarity and firmness? Certainly his
first reaction was anything but calm; he was on the point
of fainting. But he is able to exert rational control; and,
when he does so, intellectual, emotional, and physical parts
of his personality operate together ("mind, heart, and eyes
were clear"); his decision is the right one in the circumstances.

He knows that he has acted criminally, under the military code, in falling asleep at his post. This is something
"inglorious," as he himself realizes; if discovered and captured, he would be court-martialed and executed in dis-
grace. Should this happen, how would his father react?
Given the older Druse's exalted notion of honor, such a
fate for his son would be a terrible burden for him to
shoulder. Between living with a stained scutcheon or dying
to keep it untarnished, which would he have chosen? The
answer is clear to the young sentinel. To spare his father at
this moment would be no reprieve; the horseman has obviously seen the Federal soldiers in the valley below. If he
lived to report them, Carter's defection would be apparent;
and he would be meted the punishment his dereliction de-
served. The older man would live on in shame, the family

dishonored by the faithless son.

His father's parting words ring in Carter's ears: "Whatever may occur, do what you conceive to be your duty." Something horrifying has occurred, but the son's duty is plain, not only by his own standards, but by those of every soldier, Union or Confederate. Although his father must die, and by his hand, he cannot quite bring himself to aim at the horseman; instead, he shoots the mount. He knows that his father, though an enemy, is as brave as himself, and will die gloriously. And the older man does; his last moments are magnificent. Falling to his death, he yet retains his noble carriage and remains firm in the saddle. A Federal officer who observes his flight through the air is so dazed "by the apparent grace and ease and intention of the marvelous performance that it did not occur to him that the line of march of aërial cavalry is directly downward." Consequently, he wastes half an hour searching for the body at a point—according to mathematical calculations the reader can make for himself—about a quarter of a mile away from the foot of the ridge.

The reader learns in Section IV that it was well Carter Druse made the choice he did. In Section I, the narrator says that from the ridge to the valley below is a distance of over a thousand feet. But this measures the sheer drop down a cliff face. From the valley, a steeply ascending, winding mountain road would cover a distance more like fifteen hundred feet. To climb it, then, would normally take a healthy man anywhere from forty-five minutes to an hour.

But, in fact, what happens? "Ten minutes had hardly passed" after the shot when a Federal sergeant appears at Carter's side. Consequently, he must have been sent from the camp to replace the sentry—or perhaps to check up on him—long before the shot. If Druse had not fired, the sergeant would undoubtedly have seen the horseman poised on the rock, examining the tiny blue figures in the field below. The sergeant would, therefore, have had to prefer charges against his young private. As the story concludes, however, the sergeant is merely shocked at the terrible decision Carter Druse had been forced to make.

If the reader turns back now to the conclusion of Section III, he learns that, some twenty minutes after the dia-

logue between the sergeant and the private, the scouting
Federal officer concludes that his half-hour search for the
horseman's body has been in vain. He regards what he has
seen as "an incredible truth," and does not report it. He
even goes so far as to say that "there is no road leading
down into this valley from the southward." This statement,
of course, is completely false, for it is this road that Carter
Druse had traversed to take up his post, and which the sergeant has also been ordered to ascend. Consequently, "the
commander, knowing better, smiled."

At this point, I should like to refer to a long, careful
discussion of "A Horseman in the Sky" by Lawrence
Berkove,[8] whose analysis differs significantly from my own,
and is based on the assumption that the story in the *Collected Works* is merely a revision of the original *Examiner*
one, which appeared in April, 1889, and from which
Berkove quotes extensively. In the first version, Carter
Druse is clearly driven mad by the choice he has had to
make. But all the evidence for this interpretation was re-
moved by Bierce before his story appeared between covers.
Consequently, after he wrote the tale, Bierce revised it radically because, I suggest, a terrible event in his own life had
broadened and deepened his philosophy, and had shown
him the shallowness of the original version. In July, 1889,
only a few months after the appearance of "A Horseman in
the Sky" in the *Examiner*, Bierce's sixteen-year-old son was
killed in a squalid shooting-match over a girl. Bierce, strick-
en by the boy's death, is reported to have said "You did
just right, Day."

In *King Henry the Sixth, Part III*, Act II, Scene v, a son
kills his father in battle, then says: "How will my mother
for a father's death/Take on with me, and ne'er be satisfied!" This play may have been familiar to Bierce, who
knew his Shakespeare; if so, it is perhaps significant that in
the same scene it is also revealed a father has killed his son.

Bierce had learned, from the tragic experience of his own
life, that it was possible to survive the most shocking loss
and still retain one's reason. And I suggest that this knowledge, gained with such excruciating pain, caused him to re-
examine "A Horseman in the Sky." Berkove is able to give
only a rather weak explanation for the changes: according
to him, in the revised form, Bierce "left it up to the

thoughtful reader to draw his own conclusions," whereas, in the *Examiner* edition, he was "not yet willing to leave so much up to the reader."

The change is, however, fundamental; and it reflects a striking positive augmentation of Bierce's philosophy: the necessity of right thinking for right feeling. Nowhere is this made more explicit than in the last year of his life, when he wrote an introduction to Josephine McCrackin's volume of short stories in which he said: "A great writer has said that life is a farce to him who thinks, a tragedy to him who feels. But he who most deeply thinks most keenly feels; so his are the high lights and the black shadows; and however he move among them—with passive acceptance or dissenting activity—his life is more than a life: it is a career. Its every feature is 'out of the common,' and all its mutations are memorable."[9] Both Druses prefer death to shame; Carter knows his father would rather die than have their name dishonored. This is why the young private can be calm once he has thought the situation through.

Bierce was profoundly influenced by La Rochefoucauld, one of whose Maxims (No. 217) Berkove quotes, saying that it has "striking relevance" to "A Horseman in the Sky": "Intrepidity is unusual strength of soul which raises it above the troubles, disorders, and emotions that might be stirred up in it by the sight of great danger. This is the fortitude by which heroes keep their inner peace and preserve clear use of their reason in the most terrible and overwhelming crises." But, because this is clearly not applicable to Berkove's interpretation of "A Horseman in the Sky," he is forced to say that the story may be taken as a commentary which is "not necessarily acquiescent" on the maxim.[10] According to the revised version analyzed here, however, the story is a clear, straightforward dramatization of the maxim, and in complete accord with Bierce's 1913 statement quoted above.

Furthermore, Druse's psychological state finds an analogue in that endured by a modern marine. In a brief self-analysis, he writes:

> In ... any type of severe combat, time is indistinguishable. I may have remained immobile for minutes or only seconds. It was an enormous effort to move anything but my eyes; limbs were leaden as in a nightmare .... [Terror] is a rare emotion

in this age. Every soldier that has been in combat must have
felt it. The immediate problem is to overcome it as quickly as
possible. If he cannot, he ceases to function as a soldier. I
sweated profusely from the summer heat, and yet I was very
cold and shivering convulsively. After an interminable period I
overcame the thing . . . .[11]

"A Horseman in the Sky," then, is a tragic tale whose
protagonist—the gallant, high-minded Carter Druse—has to
make a terrible moral choice after a searing ordeal. But he
has the mind and heart to make it and to endure and live
with it. He is better than most, for his only mistake was to
fall asleep; yet he has to commit a deed—killing his father
—out of all proportion to his "crime." That he is able, after
his initial emotional shock, so quickly and rationally to
analyze the situation in the light of his father's character and
his own is a powerful tribute not only to man's heroism but
to his capacity for clear thinking at a moment of crisis.

In all Bierce's mimetic tales of moral choice, we have characters faced with agonizing decisions which usually involve,
as in the three stories analyzed here, death to themselves or
to those dear to them. In such a tale as "The Affair of
Coulter's Notch," the protagonist is a victim of exigencies he
does not understand; hence his choice is forced upon him.
But, if he and the colonel had had more knowledge, the
outcome might have been very different. In "A Horseman in
the Sky," however, the protagonist, in full awareness, makes
the choice that only someone capable of the most profound
thinking could have made; and, under the circumstances, it is
the wisest choice possible. The reader is left with a feeling of
deep admiration for such a man, at the same time that he
pities him and fears the possibility of an equally frightful
choice for himself.

CHAPTER 11

Mimetic Tales of Action

IN Bierce's mimetic tales of action, the protagonist acts in relation to his situation; although there may be concomitant changes in his thoughts and feelings and in his moral character, the emphasis is on what he does. The particular species to which any given story in this group belongs depends upon the emotional effect it arouses in the reader. In this chapter three mimetic tales of action are analyzed; they belong to three different literary species: "Jupiter Doke, Brigadier-General" (a tale of the absurd), "A Watcher by the Dead" (a tale of retributive tragedy), and "The Suitable Surroundings" (a terror tale).

I *Tales of the Absurd*

"Jupiter Doke, Brigadier-General"[1] is a fine example of Bierce's absurd mimetic tales of action (others are "The Widower Turmore," "My Favorite Murder," and "An Imperfect Conflagration"). Prior to an examination of this story, however, it is necessary to pay a little more attention to the form, which has been generally neglected or inadequately analyzed.

Bierce's absurd mimetic tales of action force a reexamination of accepted values in human and social ties, including family relationships; and in the operation of such institutions as the military establishment, law and the courts, medicine, business, and government. This aim is accomplished primarily by three methods: a reversal of genuine standards, hyperbolic exaggeration, and understatement. All these devices are used to create a framework so far-fetched that the reader must examine the values he thinks he holds and consider how far human practice often veers from the ideal. In every case the tales present an outrageous and unqualified deflection from accepted norms by egocentric and amoral characters who are callously insensitive to the finer emotions and who are motivated primarily by expediency, cupidity, or sadism; yet the

131

reader reacts by asking himself how far the ordinarily un-
questioned day-to-day practice also swerves from the standards to which society pays lip service.

The perversion of genuine values may include a complete
absence of any but the most aberrant ties among members of
a family, an inhuman relationship calmly taken for granted
by them; the acceptance of brutality, mayhem, and murder
as a normal way of life; or fraud, chicanery, and exploitation
described by their perpetrators not with shame but with
pride in their own cleverness. Vladimir Nabokov's *Lolita* is a
modern example of such an attitude. Often a cliché is reversed as an indication of this topsy-turvy point of view; for
example, in "The City of the Gone Away," the narrator says
that he was born "of poor because honest parents."

Intemperate exaggeration occurs in "My Favorite Murder"
when a pugnacious ram flies through the air in an arc thirty
yards long and forty or fifty feet high. Conversely, understatement is frequently a feature of these stories. In "Oil of
Dog," a fight to the death between husband and wife is called
a "disagreeable instance of domestic infelicity"; their killing
of each other, "a heedless act." In "An Imperfect Conflagration," the narrator's murder of his father "made," he says, "a
deep impression on me at the time." The reader is reminded
of the use of the same device by Jonathan Swift, whom
Bierce greatly admired, in such works as *A Modest Proposal*
and *A Tale of a Tub*, Section IX, in which Swift's persona
writes: "Last week I saw a woman flayed, and you will hardly believe how much it altered her person for the worse."

Bierce's tales of the absurd are not necessarily in the comic
mode; indeed, they may use the horrible pushed to a ludi-
crous extreme. However, "Jupiter Doke, Brigadier-General,"
does utilize the comic to demonstrate absurdity. In this story
corruption, nepotism, incompetence, and chance are presented as the normal ingredients of military, governmental,
and journalistic affairs. Doke's appointment as brigadier-
general, the conduct of his one campaign, and its aftermath
are represented in an impersonal and objective fashion
through the medium of letters, a diary, a newspaper editorial,
a Congressional resolution, and the brief statement of an un-
lettered Negro, Hannibal Alcazar Peyton, who gives the one
accurate—and completely ignored—account of the crucial incident of the narrative. As if to underline the absurdity of the

situation, Peyton's statement has fared no better in the hands of a modern editor. Although essential to an understanding of the tale, it is incomprehensibly left out of the version of "Jupiter Doke, Brigadier-General," which is included in William McCann's *Ambrose Bierce's Civil War.*[2]

The story begins when, for obviously political reasons, the Honorable Jupiter Doke, of Hardpan Crossroads, Posey County, Illinois, is proffered a Union commission as brigadier-general of volunteers. Doke, a windy rural ward heeler, assumes that a committee will be sent to inform him of his appointment; while awaiting its arrival, he writes effusively to the Secretary of War, mentioning that "the patronage of [his] office will be bestowed with an eye single to securing the greatest good to the greatest number, the stability of republican institutions and the triumph of the party in all elections."

The letters of the Secretary of War and of Major-General Blount Wardorg, to whose command Doke is assigned, are terse and to the point, however. Having been encumbered with this political appointee, they attempt to make such use of Doke as they can. The Secretary of War informs him that "the formality of official notification" by a committee must be dispensed with; that he is to proceed at once to Distilleryville, Kentucky, on the north side of the Little Buttermilk River; and that he is to take command of the Illinois Brigade there. He is to report by letter to General Wardorg, who is at Louisville.

Both the Confederates and the Federals in this area have a complicated strategy. On the south side of the Little Buttermilk, an army of twenty-five thousand rebels has been amassed. They plan to capture Covington, a three-days' march north of Distilleryville, "destroy Cincinnati and occupy the Ohio Valley." Although Distilleryville and Covington are held by the Federals, the route in between (through Bluegrass, Opossum Corners, and Horsecave[3]) has been abandoned to Southern guerrillas; and the brigade at Distilleryville is supplied by steamboats up the Little Buttermilk.

The Union strategy is to hold Distilleryville with a merely token force whose presence may induce the Confederates to strengthen their position on the south side of the river by transferring troops from Memphis, Tennessee, which the Federals plan to capture. Since the Illinois Brigade is in a very

weak position, it is to withdraw at the first sign of trouble.
But the Confederates have not disturbed it, wishing to create
the impression their own forces are small at that point.

The Secretary of War has a clever and extremely ruthless
plan to eliminate the new general before he assumes command, however. Doke is ordered to proceed secretly to
Covington, but then to travel openly and in full uniform to
Distilleryville. He does not know that this route is "infested
with bushwackers"; had he followed orders, he would probably not have reached his destination alive. But the plan
promptly founders on Doke's military inexperience and political maneuvering. When he gets to Covington on December
6, he sends his wife's cousin, Joel Briller, to Distilleryville as
his proxy, while he remains in Covington to "deliver some
addresses to the people in a local contest involving issues of
paramount importance. That duty being performed," he says
in a grand mixed metaphor, he will "in person enter the arena
of armed debate and move in the direction of the heaviest
firing, burning [his] ships behind" him. Meanwhile, he writes
the President to request that his son be designated postmaster
at Hardpan, asking the Secretary of War to "give the application a strong oral indorsement, as the appointment is in the
line of reform." He also asks what "the emoluments of the
office" he holds "in the military arm" will be, including
salary, fees, and "perquisites"; and he announces that his
"mileage account will be transmitted monthly."

Briller is never heard from again. On January 11, Doke
himself duly arrives in Distilleryville and puts up at the Henry
Clay Hotel, where he receives the three colonels in charge of
his regiments. In speeches, "the gentlemen composing the
delegation unanimously reaffirmed their devotion to the principles of national unity and the Republican party," and Doke
held a banquet for them. The next day he wrote "Mr.
Wardorg" for instructions, saying that Briller had "doubtless
been sacrificed upon the altar of his country. In him the
American people lose a bulwark of freedom." He suggests
that Wardorg "designate a committee to draw up resolutions
of respect to his memory, and that the office holders and
men under [Wardorg's] command wear the usual badge of
mourning for thirty days." He adds that "the militant De-
mocrats on the other side of the river appear to be contemplating extreme measures" and that "some of them came

down to the water's edge and remained in session for some time, making infamous allegations."

On January 13 Doke leases a "prominent residence," whose owner is away fighting for the Confederacy, for one year and sends home "for Mrs. Brigadier-General Doke and the vital issues," except for the prospective postmaster. He believes there are only three thousand Confederates across the river, and indicates that his own troops, many of whom have gone AWOL, number about two thousand. He then writes the President, asking that "the contract to supply this command with firearms and regalia" be awarded to his brother-in-law, "prominently identified with the manufacturing interests of the country."

When a battery of artillery reinforcements arrive in Jayhawk, three miles north of Distilleryville, Doke marches his entire brigade to Jayhawk to escort them into town. Their "chairman," however, mistakes the brigade for Confederates and fires at them. Doke's horse, frightened, unseats him. His men flee in disarray to Distilleryville, where they discover that the Confederates have raided the camp in their absence. Doke promptly applies for the governorship of the Idaho Territory. (Actually, what he asks for is the "Gubernatorial Chair." A clue to his character is furnished by Bierce's entry under GUBERNATORIAL in *Write It Right*: "Eschew it; it is not English, is needless and bombastic. Leave it to those who call a political office a 'chair.' 'Gubernatorial chair' is good enough for them. So is hanging.")

Nevertheless, Doke makes journalistic hay out of the fiasco; he sends a garbled account to the Posey *Maverick*, which prints it along with a fulsome editorial:

> The brilliant exploit marks an era in military history, and as General Doke says, "lays broad and deep the foundations of American prowess in arms." As none of the troops engaged, except the gallant author-chieftain (a host in himself) hails from Posey County, he justly considered that a list of the fallen would only occupy our valuable space to the exclusion of more important matter, but his account of the strategic ruse by which he apparently abandoned his camp and so inveigled a perfidious enemy into it for the purpose of murdering the sick, the unfortunate *countertempus* at Jayhawk, the subsequent dash upon a trapped enemy flushed with a supposed success, driving their terrified legions across an impassable river which

precluded pursuit—all these "moving accidents by flood and field" are related with a pen of fire and have all the terrible interest of romance.

General Wardorg on January 22 writes Doke as follows: "Your letter apprising me of your arrival at Distilleryville was delayed in transmission, having only just been received (open) through the courtesy of the Confederate department commander under a flag of truce. He begs me to assure you that he would consider it an act of cruelty to trouble you, and I think it would be. Maintain, however, a threatening attitude, but at the least pressure retire. Your position is simply an outpost which it is not intended to hold." He then writes the Secretary of War that he cannot be responsible for the "small brigade of raw troops" under Doke: "I think him a fool."

But the wily Secretary of War sees another opportunity to eliminate the bothersome general, and writes Wardorg: "The President has great faith in General Doke. If your estimate of him is correct, however, he would seem to be singularly well placed where he now is, as your plans appear to contemplate a considerable sacrifice for whatever advantages you expect to gain."

Doke, meanwhile, undismayed by Wardorg's blunt letter, moves his headquarters to Jayhawk and appoints "a Committee on Retreat," the minutes of whose first meeting he forwards. He adds: "You will perceive that the committee having been duly organized by the election of a chairman and secretary, a resolution (prepared by myself) was adopted, to the effect that in case treason again raises her hideous head on this side of the river every man of the brigade is to mount a mule, the procession to move promptly in the direction of Louisville and the loyal North." To this end, he has collected twenty-three hundred mules and penned them in a field at Jayhawk.

Nor have the Confederates been idle. On February 2 their entire force on the south side of the Little Buttermilk forded the river "three miles above Distilleryville and moved obliquely down and away from the stream, to strike the Covington turnpike at Jayhawk." As the Distilleryville brigade would then be isolated, the Confederates planned to capture it. However, as they reach Jayhawk, Doke's Negro servant, recognizing Southern voices, wakes Doke and tells him: "Skin outer dis fo' yo' life!" The frightened brigadier-general leaps out the window and rushes across the mule patch in his nightshirt.

The terrified mules break loose and thunder five abreast down the upper ford road, straight into the advancing Confederates, who are driven in confusion back to the river. There the raw Illinois troops wreak further havoc before the few remaining disorganized Confederates can cross the Little Buttermilk. Major-General Simmons B. Flood, their commander, is killed. So is the commander of the first division of fifteen thousand infantry, Major-General Gibeon J. Buxter, but not before he reports casualties of 14,994 and attributes the holocaust to a tornado. Major-General Dolliver Billows, commander of the second division of 11,200, is also killed; first, however, he reports losses of 11,199, and adds that he ferried his division across the Little Buttermilk "on two fence rails lashed together with a suspender." He attributes the losses to Union reinforcements of fifty thousand cavalry. Brigadier-General Schneddeker Baumschank, in command of a brigade of artillery, reports that "somdings occur, I know nod vot it vos—somdings mackneefcent, but it vas nod vor." He adds that his brigade was a total loss, and resigns from the Confederate Army.

On February 15, Congress passes a resolution of thanks to "Brigadier-General Jupiter Doke and the gallant men under his command for their unparalleled feat of attacking—themselves only 2000 strong—an army of 25,000 men and utterly overthrowing it." The President is requested to declare a day of thanksgiving and to appoint Doke a major-general.

This tale, it will be seen, presents a highly exaggerated account of such military inefficiency and corruption as did in fact exist during the Civil War. The Secretary of War, saddled with a political wind-bag, ruthlessly attempts to dispose of him in a way that will not be betrayed by the official correspondence; but his plans are thwarted by Doke's bumbling incompetence. The Confederates' masterly strategy is foiled by the same chance. Ironically, Wardorg, who correctly evaluates Doke's character, is proved "wrong" by the course of events. And the cowardly, stupid, greedy, and corrupt Doke emerges as a national hero and is rewarded by a promotion. Absurd though this story is, it throws upon a screen, enlarged to a size bigger than life, actual conditions. And it is the wry recognition of its blown-up correlation with reality that makes the tale amusing and provocative. Moreover, it forces a reconsideration of the very nature of war, in which chance looms so large that the most carefully thought-out plans are circumvented, not by superior military skill, but by mere luck.

II   *"A Watcher by the Dead"—Tale of Retributive Tragedy*

"A Watcher by the Dead"[4] exemplifies a very different kind of mimetic tale of action. The influence of racial memory in inspiring an antipathy to dead bodies, which in "A Tough Tussle" was used by Brainerd Byring to try to explain away his own fear, is elevated to a universal principle in this tale of retributive tragedy.

The development of the plot, which is represented in five sections, is not made clear until the conclusion of the story. Then the price paid by all four characters who have participated in a light-hearted practical joke is revealed. Two of them—Helberson, a doctor, and Harper, a medical student—have fled from San Francisco, their careers blasted; appropriately, they have become gamblers, since a harebrained bet had brought disaster upon them. A third—Dr. Mancher—has lost his wits when his attempt to aggravate the effect of a supposed corpse on an observer backfired. The fourth, Jarette, died because of his misplaced confidence that he was an exception to the general rule enunciated by Dr. Helberson: "The superstitious awe with which the living regard the dead . . . is hereditary and incurable." Under "the right conditions"—being "locked up all night with a corpse—alone—in a dark room—of a vacant house"—any man would go mad.

Young Harper mentions a fearless betting friend who would be willing to wager on his courage in such a situation, and Helberson takes the bet. By an odd coincidence, Jarette, Harper's friend, closely resembles Dr. Mancher—the coolest and most skeptical of the three physicians, who has already disclaimed for himself any share in the "superstitious feeling" Helberson had said was universal. Not wanting to be left out of the wager, Mancher volunteers to be the corpse. His two companions greet his proposal with laughter, but, portentously, the narrator immediately characterizes their plans as a "crazy conversation." Indeed, Helberson has misgivings about the scheme as it is being proposed to Jarette. But Jarette's irritatingly contemptuous manner impels the senior physician to go ahead with the plot.

Not only does the room selected for the experiment fulfill all Helberson's conditions; it adds two more. It is absolutely silent, for it does not face the street but a high breast of rock at the rear of the house. Moreover, both windows are barred. At nine o'clock Jarette is locked in this room with Mancher's sheet-covered "corpse" lying on a table. Initially, Jarette seems to justify Harper's confidence in his steel nerves; for half an hour he reads by the light of a candle, "discharging his trust with intelligence and composure." Nevertheless, he glances from time to time at the body.

Then he evinces more definite signs of unease: he gets up; inspects the corpse; and, wishing to conserve the bit of candle, blows it out with the half-formed thought that "if the situation became insupportable it would be better to have a means of relief." Almost immediately these vague symptoms of discomposure become more pronounced. He discovers that he cannot fall asleep. Wide awake, he sits in his chair unable to move, rationalizing his paralysis by telling himself that, if he groped about in the dark, he might bruise himself and disturb the body.

But now Mancher makes a faint sound. Stiff with fright, Jarette holds his breath until he grows giddy: "There was a strange ringing in his ears; his head seemed bursting; his chest was oppressed by the constriction of his clothing." As he gasps for air, he realizes the cause of his vertigo, and it leaves him. He gets up and strides about the room, overturning the furniture. Ominously, he begins talking to himself. He lights the candle, tries the locked door, and looks at his watch. It is half past nine. All these activities have consumed but a few moments. Astonished, Jarette reacts with the common gesture of holding the watch to his ear; it has not stopped.

For Bierce, an "unnatural exaltation of the senses" might commute a moment "into unthinkable cycles of time,"[5] an idea that bore its most remarkable literary fruit in "An Occurrence at Owl Creek Bridge." But in "A Watcher by the Dead," if the reader is aware of the psychological significance for Bierce of this slowing up of subjective time, he has yet another clue to Jarette's mind which forebodes disaster. The narrator understates his condition: "Mr. Jarette was not at

his ease; he was distinctly dissatisfied with his surroundings."
But he quickly passes to "anguish of . . . spirit" against which
he tries to defend himself by the same rationalizations Byring
had used in "A Tough Tussle": "what! shall I, who have not
a shade of superstition in my nature—I, who have no belief in
immortality—I, who know (and never more clearly than now)
that the after-life is the dream of a desire—shall I lose at once
my bet, my honor and my self-respect, perhaps my reason,
because certain savage ancestors dwelling in caves and bur-
rows conceived the monstrous notion that the dead walk by
night?"

His meditation is interrupted by the sound of footfalls.

From here on, the action is not represented directly, but
the reader can easily infer what happens. Jarette, in his terror, has been speaking aloud; and Mancher decides to
"'resurrect' himself." Harper and Helberson had feared that
Jarette might kill him under these circumstances. But their
fear was based on a wrong assumption: that Mancher would
reveal his identity to save Jarette. What actually happens is
that Mancher, "overhearing [Jarette] talking to himself," realizes that he is "badly frightened" and cannot "resist the
temptation to come to life and have a bit of fun out of him."
This ill-judged attempt to give their practical joke an extra
fillip backfires, however, and Jarette dies of terror.

Mancher then finds himself in the position he had coolly
claimed to be impervious to: he is alone at night with a
corpse, locked in a dark room in a deserted house. He ex-
changes clothes with Jarette and lays the genuine corpse on
the table in the position he himself originally occupied. But
he is imprisoned for six hours; as the reader learns later,
Jarette's death took place at about ten o'clock; and his body
is not discovered until four the next morning. As the minutes
drag on, Mancher's hair whitens, and he finally goes mad.
Hammering on the door in his insane fright, he is eventually
overheard as the dawn traffic stirs. When he is released, he
savagely beats his way through the gathering crowd in which
Helberson and Harper have mingled; pale, wild-eyed and
disheveled, he is an appalling spectacle. His friends assume he
is Jarette as he springs past them. That afternoon, aghast at
the outcome of their scheme, Helberson and Harper flee to
Europe.

But not until seven years later, when they meet and identi-

fy the mad Mancher, do they realize the true outcome of
their attempt to disprove what is presented in the story as a
universal truth. Jarette, whose flaw was a fatal overconfi-
dence in his ability to withstand the psychological pressures
applied to him, has died. Mancher, who not only shared his
hubris but also sought to play upon Jarette's fears for the
sake of a gruesomely inappropriate joke, has surrendered his
own reason as a consequence of the very terrors he sought to
exploit in Jarette. Helberson and Harper, who have sacrificed
their careers for a "mad wager," wind up as gamblers. This,
then, is a tale of retributive tragedy; the reader, while recognizing that the characters are not wicked men, yet appre-
ciates the justice of the retribution visited upon their heads
for their gross attempt to play foolish tricks with the human
psyche.

"A Watcher by the Dead" leans heavily upon the coincidence of Mancher's physical similarity to Jarette. Bierce, who
was greatly interested in questions of resemblance, accounted
for them on genealogical grounds which present-day geneti-
cists are only beginning to examine. His other writings indicate that he himself would have explained Jarette's and
Mancher's extraordinary similarity—not only physical but
mental and emotional—in terms of a remote common ancestor whose traits are reproduced in each. He explores the
"amazing field" of heredity and some of the strange phenomena it accounts for in an essay, "The Ancestral Bond."[6]
And he uses the theory in various ways in such stories as
"Beyond the Wall," "John Bartine's Watch," "The Death of
Halpin Frayser," and—especially—"One of Twins."[7]

III   *"The Suitable Surroundings"—Terror Tale*

Like "A Watcher by the Dead," "The Suitable Surroundings"[8] involves a solitary figure placed at night in
frightening circumstances, but it is a story of terror. Its most
interesting structural feature is the extremely complicated
relation between the chronology of the incidents and their
representation in print. Although Berkove[9] in his analysis is
certainly correct in establishing that this is not a tale of the
supernatural, and makes some headway in attacking the problem of the real action, he does not pursue far enough the
convoluted chain of events which both accounts for the victim's death and inspires the reader with the sense of terror he

does in fact feel. Like many of Bierce's stories, this one deals with an abnormal mental state—not, in this instance, a common neurosis but an out-and-out psychosis—an understanding of which is essential.

Considered chronologically, the action begins when a certain Charles Breede took his life at midnight on July 15 in "his little house in the Copeton woods," an isolated spot about ten miles from Cincinnati. At the inquest, his death was attributed to "temporary insanity." His suicide had a tremendous effect on his best friend, journalist James R. Colston. Whether the suicide was the result of a pact between the two men, as Colston comes to believe, the reader has no way of knowing; his only evidence is the statement of an obvious psychotic. What seems likelier is that Colston did know more about the circumstances of Breede's suicide than he revealed at the inquest, and that he felt increasingly accountable for it. Such an assumption is in line with psychoanalytic theory: an unbalanced person may, against all evidence, unwarrantably consider himself responsible for the death of someone close to him, particularly if he feels some guilt about any aspect of his relationship with the dead person.

Be that as it may, with the passing of time Colston believes more and more strongly that he must expiate Breede's death by taking his own life. This idea becomes an obsession with him, and it is especially fervent every July 15. Four years go by, and Colston's mania grows steadily worse. Although outwardly he has been living a normal life "destitute of adventure and action," writing journalism and fiction (especially tragic tales and ghost stories), and has established a local reputation as a writer, his "mental career has been lurid with experiences such as kill and damn." On the morning of the fourth anniversary of Breede's death, he is in an especially wild state. He boards a street car at dawn. The only other passenger is an acquaintance of his, Willard Marsh, a Babbitt who is the very acme of normality, sharing all the tastes and prejudices of his class.

Marsh is immersed in reading Colston's latest literary effort, a ghost story in the morning *Messenger*, when he is roused by the author's touch on his shoulder. Marsh greets his friend affably, telling him of his absorption in the tale. Colston, however, far from being pleased, seems annoyed; and he speaks with growing irritation, telling Marsh that, as a reader, he has "duties corresponding to his privileges." One of these is to give his "undivided attention" in a "frame of mind appropriate to the sentiment of the piece." To this end, a ghost story should be read "in solitude—at night—by the light of a candle."

While talking, Colston has been growing more and more agitated. His state seems out of all proportion to the grievance which excited it. And he uses terms to Marsh which can be described only as increasingly provocative insults, calling his friend's attitude "immoral," grossly unjust, and "infamous." His appearance and behavior are as strange as his words: his face is "uncommonly pale," his eyes glow "like living coals," and he crowds his words impetuously together. Marsh notes all these manifestations, but he does not interpret them correctly. The flaw in his reasoning is fatal, for ultimately it leads to his own death.

He fails to recognize Colston's condition for what it is because he is "a plain business man" who thinks "writers are a queer lot." He "narrowly eyed his companion, who was reported, like most men of uncommon literary ability, to be addicted to various destructive vices." That this judgment is not to be taken at face value is indicated, however, by a commentary of the narrator's which follows it immediately: "That is the revenge which dull minds take upon bright ones in resentment of their superiority. Mr. Colston was known as a man of genius. There are honest souls who believe that genius is a mode of excess." Marsh, as he continues his cogitations, dismisses the possibility that Colston, a teetotaler, could be drunk. However, since "many said that he ate opium," Marsh assumes that the writer's condition—"a certain wildness of the eyes, an unusual pallor, a thickness and rapidity of speech"—is a confirmation of the rumor.

By now, however, Marsh has grown interested in a subject which "he had not the self-denial to abandon," regardless of the fact that it has obviously plunged his friend into abnormal pique. Besides, Colston has already accused him of being dishonorable in an innuendo that makes the straightforward Marsh wince. Consequently, he forges ahead: "Do you mean to say . . . that if I . . . place myself in the conditions that you demand: solitude, night and a tallow candle—you can with your ghostly work . . . accelerate my pulse, make me start at sudden noises, send a nervous chill along my spine

and cause my hair to rise?" This may have been all that
Colston had in mind originally, but his condition has become
so exacerbated by the conversation that, in an access of
megalomania, he announces contemptuously that Marsh is a
coward whom he could kill with a manuscript. Marsh, knowing himself a brave man, is stung by the taunt; and he agrees
to read the manuscript by candlelight alone in a deserted
house in a forest that night. He does not realize it, but he has
just delivered himself over to a madman.

Colston's reaction, which seems so inexplicable to Marsh,
is understandable enough if one is aware of his condition.
Thinking himself responsible for one man's death, he compul-
sively believes he can repeat the performance. He is to produce a manuscript that night; although he announces it is in
his pocket at the moment, the reader has only his word that
it has already been prepared. In any event, whether he goes
home and writes it, or whether he already had it, sometime
during the course of the day he prepares a postscript. The
manuscript, supposedly written a week before, outlines a suicide pact between himself and Charles Breede, the one Breede
fulfilled four years earlier at midnight on July 15. Colston
then announces that he himself is going to commit suicide at
midnight on the coming July 15. The postscript adds that the
manuscript will serve to explain the death of Marsh, and that
Colston's ghost will call on him after midnight to make sure
the businessman has fulfilled the covenant.

Colston then takes Marsh to Breede's solitary little dwelling, reputed to be haunted, and leaves this strange paper with
him as the "story." When the writer returns to his boarding
house, he no longer has enough balance to act in secrecy;
and, baring his throat, he begins sharpening his razor and
trying its edge by cutting the skin of his arm. His bizarre
behavior causes one of his fellow lodgers, a more perspica-
cious observer than Marsh, to call the police, whereupon
Colston becomes so violent that he has to be confined in a
straitjacket and eventually committed to a lunatic asylum.

Meanwhile, Marsh reads the crazy document he had been
presented with. Understandably, it frightens him. His easy
acceptance of the local rumors about the strangeness of
writers generally and of Colston in particular has already
established him as credulous. Nevertheless, the manuscript
doubtless would not have had the potent effect Colston

intended had it not been for two unfortunate coincidences which lend it credence. A farmer's boy, passing the deserted Breede house shortly after midnight, sees a lighted window and approaches it to investigate. He thinks Marsh, staring apprehensively at the window, is a dead man; and the boy's fear drains his face of all color as he thrusts it through the aperture. Just as his pallid countenance appears, a screech owl cries out strangely and harshly. The startled Marsh jumps up in terror, "overturning the table and extinguishing the candle." The boy flees, but Marsh is so shocked at the sight of what seemed a ghost whose visitation was to herald his own passing that, his eyes fixed in a staring grimace and his mouth dripping saliva, he falls dead.

The next day the boy leads three skeptical men to the Breede house, where they find Marsh's body and the manuscript. One of the men—Breede's son-in-law—reads the manuscript aloud, except for the part which purports to reveal Colston's connection with the Breede suicide. This excerpt, for whatever reason—conceivably, its implausibility, but certainly the unfortunate effect it would have in recalling the tragedy to Breede's daughter—he keeps to himself. He then burns the manuscript before the other men have a chance to see it, and he later placidly endures "a severe reprimand from the coroner." Significantly, his companions are unable to give an intelligent account at the inquest of the portion they had heard read aloud.

This outline is the *action* of the story, however, not its representation. It is told in five sections. The first, subtitled "The Night," gives us the point of view of a superstitious boy. He and his frightened fellows believed the Breede house —deserted after its owner's suicide—to be haunted; "to attest alike their courage and their hostility to the supernatural," they have thrown stones at the window. Now, at midnight, when the boy sees the "dim light" shining from it, he is apprehensive: "He half expected to be set upon by all the unworldly and bodiless malevolences whom he had outraged by assisting to break alike their windows and their peace." When he looks in the window, he sees what he believes is a dead man staring soullessly out; and the sight, to him, is horribly fascinating. He stops, "weak, faint and trembling; he could feel the blood forsaking his face. Nevertheless, he set his teeth and resolutely advanced to the house. He had no conscious intention—it was the mere courage of terror." At the same moment that he thrusts his white face into the window, the owl shrieks. The "corpse" springs up and, the boy believes, blows out the candle.

The second section, subtitled "The Day Before," presents the clues needed to understand Colston's condition. Although set in a workaday morning atmosphere, in the prosaic setting of a streetcar, this part suggests the really terrifying elements of the tale to the attentive reader. If he recalls Bierce's well-known love of irony, he finds this section a sardonic commentary not only on Bierce's own title but also on Colston's version of what constitutes "the suitable surroundings" for a tale of terror.

In the third section, "The Day After," the boy has told his story to the three men. They did not believe him, and he did not insist, knowing his story hardly establishes him as "a credible witness." But, when they find Marsh's body, one says: "you're a good 'un"; this is "Scepticism apologizing to Truth." But the boy's interpretation is *not* true, as Breede's son-in-law shortly discovers.

The fourth section, "The Manuscript," reveals the precipitating factors for the protagonist's psychotic state. Breede's son-in-law obviously considers that Colston's version could cast no real light on his father-in-law's death and that it would merely reopen an old wound from which his wife would needlessly suffer. The son-in-law seems perfectly normal. Would he have burned the manuscript if it could relieve Breede's name of the onus of having committed suicide while temporarily insane? In fact, neither he nor the other two men take it seriously enough to present its contents to the coroner as a plausible cause for Marsh's death.

The fifth section, "From 'The Times,'" is an account in a rival newspaper of Colston's irrational and violent behavior and of his commitment to an asylum. Bierce disguises the terrifying effect of this section by presenting it in a pseudo-humorous tone, having the *Times* reporter pretend that, of course, all the *Messenger*'s writers are insane.

This tale is one whose technique bears a certain resemblance to that of "The Death of Halpin Frayser." As in that story, the representation is carefully constructed to lure the unwary reader into believing this tale to be one of the supernatural. Many things in "The Suitable Surroundings" contribute to such a misleading assumption. There are three levels of interpretation for the action. The superstitious boy's explanation obviously cannot be trusted. In the first section, the narrator tells us that Marsh's "eyes were fixed upon the blank window space with a stare in which an older and cooler observer might have discerned something of apprehension." And, at the moment of Marsh's death, the narrator explicitly tells us that "the man sprang to his feet, overturning the table and extinguishing the candle," although the boy thinks the "dead man" has blown it out.

But these clues are traps for the unwary reader. By elevating him to a position above the boy, the narrator may trick him into accepting a second level of interpretation, that of Colston and Marsh. This is furthered by two devices: first, by giving only Colston's view of what constitutes "the suitable surroundings"; and second, by neglecting to reveal the middle portion of Colston's manuscript, thus creating an aura of mystery about it. The incautious reader is therefore subtly guided to identify himself with Marsh. Even if he understands little more of where the real terror lies than does Marsh, he still shares some of Marsh's fear. The third level of interpretation is played down by revealing Colston's true condition only through a short, humorous account drawn from a rival newspaper.

For the real terror in the story derives from its investigation of the growth of psychosis in the protagonist and from the ease with which such an unbalanced madman can play upon the ordinary prejudices and fears of a not very perceptive and rather credulous Everyman. The reader may well consider whether he himself could resist a determined, intelligent psychotic like Colston. Would he not—like Marsh—allow his actions to be controlled by a clever manipulation of his own prejudices instead of by a rational assessment of a complicated psychological condition?

Bierce's mimetic tales of action have in common protagonists who themselves initiate the events controlling the plot development. Beyond this likeness, however, one can point to no necessary formal similarities among stories of this genus; the reader's reaction will vary widely from one species to another. The astounding array of effects Bierce was able to create even within this narrow field is a magnificent encomium to the versatility on which he prided himself.

CHAPTER *12*

Dazzling Brilliants: The Short Forms

LEAVING the tale and turning to an examination of Bierce's other writing, one is struck by the large proportion in forms even briefer than the short story. Although these little works find loose parallels in the didactic and the absurd tales, further generalizations are difficult. Some of the short forms are in prose; some, in verse; some, a mixture of prose and verse. Some are narrative; some, dramatic. They range in length from one-word definitions to anecdotes and short essays. Some are *réductiones ad absurdum*, presenting the reverse of the obvious intention. Others, however, are serious statements to be taken at face value, like the poignant Epigram inspired by Bierce's own suffering: "To parents only, death brings an inconsolable sorrow. When the young die and the old live, nature's machinery is working with the friction that we name grief" (*Works*, VIII, 363). Some of the short forms indulge in self-mockery; others deal with actual persons, institutions, an entire culture, or the nature of man. Although it is possible to discern certain more-or-less constant themes running through several items, it is also possible to find those which contradict one another. As Bierce pointed out in one of his *Epigrams* (*Works*, VIII, 367): "Convictions are variable; to be always consistent is to be sometimes dishonest."

Nevertheless, four significant features of these short forms are apparent to the reader; and Bierce explicitly aimed at them: clear thinking, wit, precision, and taste. In order to understand what he meant by each of these qualities, one must turn to the short forms themselves, in which he outlined his views. Many of these attitudes about the characteristics of good writing are found in his little book *Write It Right*, a catchy title he chose for its commercial appeal. He wrote it late in life, in 1909; it is a mature statement of his

considered beliefs on style; and he told his publisher that he
felt something "more nearly like pride" in it "than in any of
[his] other work."[1]

In the Introduction to *Write It Right*, Bierce says that
"good writing . . . , essentially, is clear thinking made visible." The same idea is implicit in a satirical verse by "Sigis-
mund Smith," which is appended to the definition of
LEXICOGRAPHER in *The Devil's Dictionary* (*Works*, VII, 191).
In the Preface to *The Devil's Dictionary*, Bierce elevates sense
over sentiment—another emphasis on clear thinking. And he
"thought it needless to classify" the verses in *Shapes of Clay*;
the character of each, being readily discernible, would, he
hoped, enable the reader's mood to "accommodate itself
without disappointment to that of his author."[2]

Wit is a second characteristic of these short forms. Bierce
distinguished it from humor, to which he thought it superior,
comparing wit to a dry wine; humor, to a sweet. "Humor is
tolerant, tender," he wrote; "its ridicule caresses. Wit stabs,
begs pardon—and turns the weapon in the wound." Moreover, it does not induce laughter. "Wit may make us smile, or
make us wince," but it is "a serious matter. To laugh at it is
to confess that you do not understand." Pitilessly sharp, it is
as "bleak as steel," indicting the horrible depths of man's
soul. It is paradoxical, "not altogether true and therefore not
altogether dull," yet nevertheless "profoundly wise." It is
audacious and startling; clever, charming, and quotable. Unlike humor, wit is a universal tongue; but few can speak
it—and very few Americans. It is "the salt with which the
American humorist spoils his intellectual cookery by leaving
it out," replacing it with slang. The French, on the other
hand, notably Rochefoucauld and Rabelais, are particularly
glib in this *lingua franca*.[3]

Precision, the third notable feature of these short forms,
was to Bierce a "point of capital concern" he frequently
discussed:[4] "As Quintilian puts it, the writer should so write
that his reader not only may, but must, understand." Precision could be attained only through use of the *mot juste*, to
which dictionaries were a poor guide since they tended to
rigidify usage. Language is not static; it grows by innovation
(the invention of new words and the use of old ones in unfamiliar senses) and by the rediscovery of obsolete and obso-
lescent words which have no exact modern equivalents.

As this view of language indicates, Bierce was a linguistic liberal, not a purist. The function of dictionaries was "to make a record, not to give a law." He believed that "few words have more than one literal and serviceable meaning," which is "not always determined by derivation, and seldom by popular usage," being found neither in the "narrow etymons of the mere scholar" nor in the "loose locutions of the ignorant." "The writer who allows himself as much liberty in the use of words as he is allowed by the dictionary-maker and by popular consent is a bad writer."

The fourth and last feature of these short forms is taste, for which, as Bierce pointed out, "there are neither standards nor arbiters."[5] Inevitably, therefore, what the reader gets is Bierce's own taste; and he did not claim it was impeccable. It may be sampled in one of his *Fables from "Fun"* (*Works*, VI, 335-36):

> "I say, you," bawled a fat Ox in a stall to a lusty young Ass who was braying outside; "the like of that is not in good taste."
>
> "In whose good taste, my adipose censor?" inquired the Ass, not too respectfully.
>
> "Why—ah—h'm. I mean that it does not suit me. You should bellow."
>
> "May I ask how it concerns you whether I bellow or bray, or do both, or neither?"
>
> "I cannot tell you," said the Ox, shaking his head despondingly—"I do not at all understand the matter. I can only say that I have been used to censure all discourse that differs from my own."
>
> "Exactly," said the Ass; "you have tried to make an art of impudence by calling preferences principles. In 'taste' you have invented a word incapable of definition to denote an idea impossible of expression, and by employing the word 'good' or 'bad' in connection with it you indicate a merely subjective process, in terms of an objective quality. Such presumption transcends the limits of mere effrontery and passes into the boundless empyrean of pure gall!"
>
> The bovine critic having no words to express his disapproval of this remarkable harangue, said it was in bad taste.

These four qualities—clear thinking, wit, precision, and Bierce's own taste—are common to the jewel-hard little forms discussed in this chapter. Since they are very short, the easiest way to present them is simply to display a variety, so that the reader may weigh their carats for himself. Certain themes have a tendency to run through many of them; and, when considered together, they furnish a compendium of Bierce's beliefs on a number of subjects: international relations, politics, religion, medicine, business, and the pleasures of good food and drink. An examination of three of these themes—science, law, and the war between the sexes—furnishes both examples of the various short forms which he utilized and some idea of his attitude toward the world in which he lived.

I *Science*

Bierce's views on science may be summarized as a conservative reluctance to embrace it unthinkingly on faith. The dialogue cited below, from *Epigrams*, exemplifies this skepticism:

> "Whose dead body is that?"
> "Credulity's."
> "By whom was he slain?"
> "Credulity."
> "Ah, suicide."
> "No, surfeit. He dined at the table of Science, and swallowed all that was set before him." (*Works*, VIII, 367)

The following quotations, which are commentaries on this Epigram, are drawn from *The Devil's Dictionary*:

GRAVITATION, *n.* The tendency of all bodies to approach one another with a strength proportioned to the quantity of matter they contain—the quantity of matter they contain being ascertained by the strength of their tendency to approach one another. This is a lovely and edifying illustration of how science, having made A the proof of B, makes B the proof of A.

MOLECULE, *n.* The ultimate, indivisible unit of matter. It is distinguished from the corpuscle, also the ultimate, indivisible unit of matter, by a closer resemblance to the atom, also the ultimate, indivisible unit of matter. Three great scientific theories of the structure of the universe are the molecular, the corpuscular and the atomic. A fourth affirms, with Haeckel, the condensation or precipitation of

matter from ether—whose existence is proved by the condensation or precipitation. The present trend of scientific
thought is toward the theory of ions. The ion differs from
the molecule, the corpuscle and the atom in that it is an
ion. A fifth theory is held by idiots, but it is doubtful if
they know any more about the matter than the others.

ZOOLOGY, *n.* The science and history of the animal kingdom,
including its king, the House Fly (*Musca maledicta*). The
father of Zoölogy was Aristotle, as is universally conceded,
but the name of its mother has not come down to us. Two
of the science's most illustrious expounders were Buffon
and Oliver Goldsmith, from both of whom we learn (*L'His-
toire générale des animaux* and *A History of Animated
Nature*) that the domestic cow sheds its horns every two
years.

The definition of MONAD and the little essays, "Dethronement of the Atom" (*Works*, IX, 344-47) and "Pectolite"
(X, 379-81), are other examples of Bierce's cautious, skeptical attitude toward science.

II *Law*

A second theme that runs through many of his short works
is the law[6] as actually practiced by lawyers and judges. A
sampling of his opinions, culled from a number of sources,
gives some notion of the enormous variety of literary devices
encountered in the short forms. The first group of items are
all taken from *The Devil's Dictionary*; also relevant are the
definitions of HABEAS CORPUS, INADMISSIBLE, JUSTICE,
LITIGATION, and TRIAL. The initials "G. J." after the entry on
LAW (cited below) refer to "that learned and ingenious cleric,
Father Gassalasca Jape, S.J.," whom Bierce often "quoted"
in *The Devil's Dictionary*.

LAW, *n.*   Once Law was sitting on the bench,
              And Mercy knelt a-weeping.
           "Clear out!" he cried, "disordered wench!
              Nor come before me creeping.
           Upon your knees if you appear,
              'Tis plain you have no standing here."
           Then Justice came. His Honor cried:
              "*Your* status?—devil seize you!"
           "*Amica curiae*," she replied—

"Friend of the court, so please you."
"Begone!" he shouted—"there's the door—
I never saw your face before!"

G. J.

LAWFUL, *adj.* Compatible with the will of a judge having jurisdiction.

LAWYER, *n.* One skilled in circumvention of the law.

LIAR, *n.* A lawyer with a roving commission.

LITIGANT, *n.* A person about to give up his skin for the hope of retaining his bones.

PRECEDENT, *n.* In Law, a previous decision, rule or practice which, in the absence of a definite statute, has whatever force and authority a Judge may choose to give it, thereby greatly simplifying his task of doing as he pleases. As there are precedents for everything, he has only to ignore those that make against his interest and accentuate those in the line of his desire. Invention of the precedent elevates the trial-at-law from the low estate of a fortuitous ordeal to the noble attitude of a dirigible arbitrament.

SATAN, *n.* One of the Creator's lamentable mistakes, repented in sashcloth and axes. Being instated as an archangel, Satan made himself multifariously objectionable and was finally expelled from Heaven. Halfway in his descent he paused, bent his head in thought a moment and at last went back. "There is one favor that I should like to ask," said he.
"Name it."
"Man, I understand, is about to be created. He will need laws."
"What, wretch! you his appointed adversary, charged from the dawn of eternity with hatred of his soul—you ask for the right to make his laws?"
"Pardon; what I have to ask is that he be permitted to make them himself."
It was so ordered.

TECHNICALITY, *n.* In an English court a man named Home was tried for slander in having accused a neighbor of murder. His exact words were: "Sir Thomas Holt hath taken a cleaver and stricken his cook upon the head, so that one side of the head fell upon one shoulder and the other side upon the other shoulder." The defendant was acquitted by instruction of the court, the learned judges holding that the words did not charge murder, for they did not affirm the death of the cook, that being only an inference.

Other short forms representing Bierce's attitude toward the law are reproduced below *in toto*:

DECEASED AND HEIRS

A Man died leaving a large estate and many sorrowful relations who claimed it. After some years, when all but one had had judgment given against them, that one was awarded the estate, which he asked his Attorney to have appraised.

"There is nothing to appraise," said the Attorney, pocketing his last fee.

"Then," said the Successful Claimant, "what good has all this litigation done me?"

"You have been a good client to me," the Attorney replied, gathering up his books and papers, "but I must say you betray a surprising ignorance of the purpose of litigation."[7]

JUDGE AND PLAINTIFF

A Man of Experience in Business was awaiting the judgment of the Court in an action for damages that he had brought against a railway company. The door opened and the Judge of the Court entered.

"Well," said he, "I am going to decide your case to-day. If I should decide in your favor I wonder how you would express your satisfaction."

"Sir," said the Man of Experience in Business, "I should risk your anger by offering you one-half the sum awarded."

"Did I say I was going to decide that case?" said the Judge, abruptly, as if awakening from a dream. "Dear me, how absent-minded I am! I mean I have already decided it, and judgment has been entered for the full amount that you sued for."

"Did I say I would give you one-half?" said the Man of Experience in Business, coldly. "Dear me, how near I came to being a rascal! I mean, that I am greatly obliged to you."[8]

A DEFECTIVE PETITION

An Associate Justice of the Supreme Court was sitting by a river when a Traveler approached and said:

"I wish to cross. Will it be lawful to use this boat?"

"It will," was the reply; "it is my boat."

The Traveler thanked him, and pushing the boat into the water embarked and rowed away. But the boat sank and he was drowned.

"Heartless man!" said an Indignant Spectator. "Why did you not tell him that your boat had a hole in it?"

"The matter of the boat's condition," said the great jurist, "was not brought before me."[9]

AN ERROR

"I never have been able to determine
Just how it is that the judicial ermine
Is safely guarded from predacious vermin."
"It is not so, my friend; though in a garret
'Tis kept in camphor, and you often air it,
The vermin will get into it and wear it."[10]

Death is not the end; there remains the litigation over the estate.[11]

Another aspect of Bierce's attitude toward the law, however, is revealed in the two passages quoted below:

What theology is to religion and jurisprudence to justice, etiquette is to civility.[12]

Leading Question. A leading question is not necessarily an important one; it is one that is so framed as to suggest, or lead to, the answer desired. Few others than lawyers use the term correctly.[13]

III *The War Between the Sexes*

Still a third theme traceable through these short forms is the relation between the sexes; Bierce's comments on this topic have been widely quoted. Although these tend to be satirical and witty, a small number are to be taken at very nearly face value. Among the former group are many entries in *The Devil's Dictionary*, Epigrams, and fables. The following definitions are all from *The Devil's Dictionary*:[14]

BRIDE, *n.* A woman with a fine prospect of happiness behind her.

BRUTE, *n.* See HUSBAND.

GARTER, *n.* An elastic band intended to keep a woman from coming out of her stockings and desolating the country.

HERS, *pron.* His.

MALE, *n.* A member of the unconsidered, or negligible sex. The male of the human race is commonly known (to the female) as Mere Man. The genus has two varieties: good providers and bad providers.

MARRIAGE, *n.* The state or condition of a community consisting of a master, a mistress and two slaves, making in all, two.

QUEEN, *n.* A woman by whom the realm is ruled when there is a king, and through whom it is ruled when there is not.

Bierce's *Epigrams* (*Works*, VIII, 343-81), short, pithy observations on a variety of topics, probably include more remarks about men and women than about any other subject. A selection from these illustrates their general tenor, but there are many more:

Our vocabulary is defective; we give the same name to woman's lack of temptation and man's lack of opportunity.

Of two kinds of temporary insanity, one ends in suicide, the other in marriage.

What a woman most admires in a man is distinction among men. What a man most admires in a woman is devotion to himself.

For study of the good and bad in woman two women are a needless expense.

Woman would be more charming if one could fall into her arms without falling into her hands.

Two little fables also illustrate Bierce's satirical attitude toward the war between the sexes:

THE WITCH'S STEED

A Broomstick that had long served a witch as a steed complained of the nature of its employment, which it thought degrading.

"Very well," said the Witch, "I will give you work in which you will be associated with intellect—you will come in contact with brains. I shall present you to a housewife."

"What!" said the Broomstick, "do you consider the hands of a housewife intellectual?"

"I referred," said the Witch, "to the head of her good man."[15]

THE INCONSOLABLE WIDOW

A Woman in widow's weeds was weeping upon a grave.

"Console yourself, madam," said a Sympathetic Stranger. "Heaven's mercies are infinite. There is another man somewhere, besides your husband, with whom you can still be happy."

"There was," she sobbed—"there was, but this is his grave."[16]

Despite the cynical attitude displayed in these witty little pieces, Bierce had all his adult life an enormous number of devoted women friends. And, although in many of these brief forms he mocked the short-lived grief of widows,[17] in *The Devil's Dictionary* the following definition occurs:

> WIDOW, *n.* A pathetic figure that the Christian world has agreed to take humorously, although Christ's tenderness towards widows was one of the most marked features of his character.

And he also wrote that "A virtuous widow is the most loyal of mortals; she is faithful to that which is neither pleased nor profited by her fidelity."[18]

A very few of Bierce's short pieces about men and women are relatively straightforward, and reveal the complexity of his opinions. These comments are far-ranging. On the one hand is a bitter passage in "Music," an essay included in *Tangential Views* (*Works*, IX, 360): "The married have a tacit undertaking to wreathe their chains with flowers, smile away their wounds, and exhibit as becoming ornaments the handles of the daggers rusting in their hearts." But, on the other hand, one finds the idealism of the following couplet: "Study good women and ignore the rest, / For he best knows the sex who knows the best."[19]

Perhaps the most interesting aspect of Bierce's attitude on this subject, however, given the time in which he lived, is his frank avowal of the part sex plays in love and his disgust at contemporary blinking of the fact. This candor, expressed in a number of sources,[20] helps to account for the slight role women play in his short stories. One may note here two definitions from *The Devil's Dictionary*:

> CUPID, *n.* The so-called god of love. This bastard creation of a barbarous fancy was no doubt inflicted upon mythology for the sins of its deities. Of all unbeautiful and inappropriate conceptions this is the most reasonless and offensive. The notion of symbolizing sexual love by a semisexless babe, and comparing the pains of passion to the wounds of an arrow—of introducing this pudgy homunculus into art grossly to materialize the subtle spirit and suggestion of the work—this is eminently worthy of the age that, giving it birth, laid it on the doorstep of posterity.

> PLATONIC, *adj.* Pertaining to the philosophy of Socrates. Platonic Love is a fool's name for the affection between a disability and a frost.

IV *Fables*

An examination of the various items that have been
quoted reveals the variety of devices used: sharp definitions
in a single word or a phrase; anecdotes; puns; parody; pseudo-
learning; verse; or, often, combinations of these. My own
favorites among the short forms are the fables, in some of
which the qualities outlined at the beginning of this chapter
find their apotheosis: clear thinking, wit, precision, and
Bierce's own pungent taste. Four of these fables are cited
below and analyzed: "Hen and Vipers" and "Mountain and
Mouse" from *Aesopus Emendatus* (*Works*, VI, 348, 359); and
"The Thoughtful Warden" and "A Matter of Method" from
Fantastic Fables (VI, 174, 213-14):

HEN AND VIPERS

A Hen who had patiently hatched out a brood of vipers was
accosted by a Swallow, who said: "What a fool you are to give
life to creatures that will reward you by destroying you."

"I am a little bit destructive myself," said the Hen, tranquilly,
swallowing one of the little reptiles; "and it is not an act of folly
to provide oneself with the delicacies of the season."

MOUNTAIN AND MOUSE

A Mountain was in labor, and the people of seven cities had
descended to watch its movements and hear its groans. While they
waited in breathless expectancy out came a Mouse.

"Oh, what a baby!" they cried in derision.

"I may be a baby," said the Mouse, gravely, as he passed outward through the forest of shins, "but I know tolerably well how
to diagnose a volcano."

THE THOUGHTFUL WARDEN

The Warden of a Penitentiary was one day putting locks on the
doors of all the cells when a mechanic said to him:

"Those locks can all be opened from the inside—you are very
imprudent."

The Warden did not look up from his work, but said:

"If that is called imprudence I wonder what would be called a
thoughtful provision against the vicissitudes of fortune."

A MATTER OF METHOD

A Philosopher seeing a Fool beating his Donkey, said:

"Abstain, my son, abstain, I implore. Those who resort to
violence shall suffer from violence."

"That," said the Fool, diligently belaboring the animal, "is what I'm trying to teach this beast—which has kicked me."

"Doubtless," said the Philosopher to himself, as he walked away, "the wisdom of fools is no deeper nor truer than ours, but they really do seem to have a more impressive way of imparting it."

All of these little *jeux d'esprit* involve a dialogue between two characters and a sudden, sharp reversal of their roles. As the fable begins, the reader finds himself identifying with the character who apparently represents the voice of wisdom (the Swallow, the people, the mechanic, and the Philosopher) and who is expostulating with the character who seems an obvious nitwit (the Hen, the Mouse, the Warden, and the Fool).

The reason for this identification, according to Sergei Eisenstein in one of the best analyses yet to appear of the wit that synthesizes Bierce's short forms, is a universal psychological tendency by which one automatically (and wrongly) combines juxtaposed elements in a false unity. For example, in "The Inconsolable Widow" (quoted above), which Eisenstein cites, the juxtaposition of the grave with the woman in mourning leads the reader to infer that she is a widow weeping for her husband; in fact, she is mourning for her lover. In works of this kind, one simultaneously perceives both the new result and its independent parts, two of which one had formerly yoked together in an obvious, though erroneous, conjunction; and comic wit results.[21]

The delight with which one reacts to Bierce's fables arises from this sudden, unexpected peripety: with the roles of wit and butt reversed, the ostensible stooge calmly turns the tables on his supposedly clever interlocutor. The trapped reader realizes a moment later that the tables have also been turned on him, and he promptly realigns his sympathies, his merriment at the discomfiture of the new butt being heightened by the fact that he was, himself, momentarily taken in; and by his natural human (if not very admirable) glee at seeing those in high places tumbled from their vaunted pinnacles.

CHAPTER 13

Significance

A GRASP of the significance of Bierce, both in this country and abroad, is complicated by the fact that a great deal of what has been written about him is of little value—even, in some cases, positively misleading. Despite a few early studies of some merit, the short discussion by Harry Levin in *The Literary History of the United States*[1] is disappointingly inaccurate as an interpretation of Bierce's position in American letters. Both Levin and Emily Hahn, in her recent *Romantic Rebels*,[2] follow the same *ignis fatuus* in treating him as a "bohemian," which he was not. Moreover, two distinguished modern critics, Edmund Wilson and Van Wyck Brooks, have each written a pair of strangely contradictory essays on Bierce.

Most students have concentrated on attempts to portray his life and to interpret his complex, magnetic personality. By and large, their efforts have not been successful. Because the waters of Bierce studies have been so thoroughly roiled by writers washing their own dirty linen—notably Adolphe de Castro, Walter Neale, and even George Sterling—it is probable that future biographical investigations will have to be undertaken on the same detailed, painstaking scale that Paul Fatout employed in his excellent *Ambrose Bierce and the Black Hills*.

However, the scholars and critics of American literature, after years of superficial or even erroneous treatment, are beginning to come to grips with Bierce's life and writings. Probably the best full-length modern studies have been doctoral dissertations, but these too are of unequal quality. And a penetrating short appraisal of Bierce is made by Carey McWilliams, in an essay only a few pages long. Commenting on the fact that he is "still a peripheral figure in American literature," McWilliams adds:

> But he deserves a central niche for he was, on a number of counts, one of the most remarkable writers of his generation.
>
> . . . One might sum up the case for Bierce by saying that he wrote a half dozen of the finest American short stories, a dozen or so of the most memorable letters and battle pieces, some of the best American satiric verse and that he was the greatest American satirist in the classic tradition . . . . It is a substantial achievement, meriting a more secure niche than the academicians have ever been willing to accord.[3]

Not surprisingly, perhaps, creative writers have been rather perceptive students of Bierce. During his lifetime, Gertrude Atherton and H. L. Mencken both realized his genius; and, although they were personal friends of his, they were objective enough to keep their judgment unclouded. The young Stephen Crane, who "came to believe that *The Red Badge of Courage* was too long," deeply admired Bierce's short stories;[4] and it has been suggested that the irony of Crane's poetry derives in part from the short forms discussed in Chapter 12.[5]

Bierce's influence on the style and thought of Ernest Hemingway[6] and James Thurber has been often remarked. Not so well known is the admiration of James Agee, who wrote to Father James Harold Flye on November 26, 1937: "Bierce is good . . . . Irony and savage anger and even certain planes of cynicism are, used right, nearly as good instruments and weapons as love, and not by any means incompatible with it; good lens-wipers and good auxiliaries. In plenty of ways I care most for those who lack the easing and comfort of direct love, Swift above any; and a lot for smaller, sharp intelligent soreheads like Bierce."[7] A recent essay suggests that Dylan Thomas also borrowed heavily from Ambrose Bierce.[8]

Bierce's skill as a precursor of modern science fiction is being given increasing recognition. H. Bruce Franklin has pointed out that his work in this field has probably been relatively neglected because "it tends toward pure speculation about the forces which may, existing beyond human ken, govern man." Such stories, in the absence of "a solid tradition of this kind of fiction," have been difficult to as-

sess, dealing as they do with "inconceivable other forms of
life . . . , inconceivable psychic dimensions," and "inconceivable physical dimensions." An early explorer in the realm of
modern speculative science fiction, Bierce was, in Franklin's
view, a map maker for the uncharted area on which he had
boldly set forth.[9]

I *Political and Social Theory*

Bierce's political thinking has, on the whole, been given
short shrift. Although it has been customary to dismiss it
lightly, no really adequate study of it has yet been made. One
reason may lie in its complexity. Taking a dark view of
human nature, Bierce agreed with Tom Paine and Thoreau
that, "were the impulses of conscience clear, uniform, and
irresistibly obeyed, man would need no other lawgiver."[10]
But, unlike these earlier Americans, he followed the negative
implications of this truism to the pessimistic conclusion dem-
onstrated by history that no recorded form of government
had ever given "good and wise administration" because of
humanity's "essential folly and . . . depravity."

The only "two forms of real government" that existed,
"absolute Monarchy and absolute Democracy," were fore-
doomed to failure because of the nature of man, from which
neither kings nor populace were exempt. "Limited Monar-
chies and constitutional Democracies" were, however, no
more stable than the pure forms; moreover, they had the
added weaknesses of divided authority and divided responsibility. Although Bierce recognized the virtues of an aristocracy composed of the best and wisest men, as exemplified by
the British, he deplored the oppressed condition of the English lower classes. Nor did he make the mistake of confusing
an aristocracy with the plutocracy he abhorred, for no
Roosevelt ever denounced more stingingly the graft and corruption engendered by malefactors of great wealth.

As an egalitarian American, Bierce respected the republican ideal; but he had small faith in the practicality of its
institutions for "governing men as men are" because no re-
public could continue to repress the internal forces which
tended to its own disintegration. "Everything foretells the
doom of authority," he wrote, including the assassination of
Presidents—a phenomenon that he foresaw, with terrifying
sharpness of vision, would recur. He also anticipated proleta-

rian revolution and its transformation into dictatorship. "It is easy to forecast the first stages of the End's approach: Rioting. Disaffection of constabulary and troops. Subversion of the Government. A policy of decapitation. Parliament of the people. Divided counsels. Pandemonium. The man on horseback. Gusts of grape. ——?" This melancholy prospect was given imaginative form in his dystopias: "Ashes of the Beacon," *The Land Beyond the Blow*, "For the Ahkoond," "John Smith, Liberator," and "The Future Historian."

It is hardly accurate to say, as does Edmund Wilson in *Patriotic Gore* (628), that Bierce apparently favored monarchy as "the most satisfactory form of government." Rather, he saw every existing government as an uneasy equilibrium between authority (whether it took the form of absolute monarchy or state socialism) and anarchy. Like Aristotle, he favored some kind of mixed polity in which the various warring tensions could, for a time at least, balance one another. "The system that we have the happiness to endure" in the United States blends socialism and anarchism, lying at a point somewhere between. The practical problem was to maintain this fragile balance for as long as possible. Although he scorned the sentimental socialism of Edwin Markham, Jack London, and Upton Sinclair, many of Bierce's specific proposals for reform were to be incorporated in the modern welfare state. "The principle of public ownership," he believed, "is already accepted and established"; and the trend toward "absolute Socialism" was a conspicuous phenomenon in all civilized countries. Like many others of his time, including some whom he criticized, he favored government ownership of railroads, public employment for the needy, and some form of inheritance and progressive income taxes. He also believed that private ownership of land, the importation of cheap labor, and competitive wage systems should all be abolished.

These proposals, however, were presented as historical expedients that were not to be justified in terms of abstract theory. Seeing both strengths and weaknesses in every form of government, Bierce believed in judging each political problem on its merits without reference to a preconceived "set of solemn principles," for "what one may think perfect one may not always think desirable." Such perceptive theorists as Harold D. Lasswell and Abraham Kaplan quote approvingly

Bierce's definition of REVOLUTION as "an abrupt change in the form of misgovernment" to support the serious dialectical proposition that "the counterelite constitutes the initial elite of the new power structure."[11]

II *Letters*

Bierce's remarkable epistolary talent should also be pointed out. Unfortunately, such letters as have heretofore been published have had very limited circulation. They include two volumes of selections which were rare books almost from the day they were printed, and a few scattered letters which have appeared in articles in learned journals. Van Wyck Brooks, in a perceptive review deploring the small number of readers who could have access to even such letters as had been published, said that

> few better craftsmen in words than Bierce have lived in this country, and his letters might well have introduced him to the larger public that, even now, scarcely knows his name . . . .
>
> His outlook, as these letters reveal it, was broadly human. With his air of a somewhat dandified Strindberg he combined what might be described as a temperament of the eighteenth century. It was natural to him to write in the manner of Pope: lucidity, precision, "correctness" were the qualities he adored. He was full of the pride of individuality; and . . . was, in his personal life, the serenest of stoics . . . .
>
> . . . Sombre and at times both angry and cynical as Bierce's writing may seem, no man was ever freer from personal bitterness. If he was out of sympathy with the life of his time and with most of its literature, he adored literature itself . . . . It is this dry and at the same time whole-souled enthusiasm that makes his letters so charming . . . .
>
> In certain ways, to be sure, this is a sad book . . . . It is impossible to read his letters without feeling that he was a starved man; but certainly it can be said that, if his generation gave him very little, he succeeded in retaining in his own life the poise of an Olympian.[12]

The collected edition of his letters now being prepared by the author of this study will reveal Bierce as one of the great masters of the epistolary form. The clarity of his other writings, which was basically a quality of mind, appears also in his letters. And the engaging warmth and intimacy of many of them reveal an aspect of his character—that of the kindly friend—which has been almost totally obscured by such sobriquets as "Bitter Bierce," "The Devil's Lexicographer," and "The Wickedest Man in San Francisco." In addition, his own side of some of the quarrels about which the public has heard much from his antagonists sets them in a very different light from the customary version.

III *International Recognition*

The most interesting aspect of Bierce's increasing fame is the slow and steady growth of his reputation abroad, which began, of course, in England, where his first three books were published. It continued with an early perceptive essay by Eric Partridge[13] and with outspoken praise in the London *Times Literary Supplement* for September 17, 1954,[14] which cited him as an authentic voice in the development of a distinctively American style, "a clear, sure craftsman" who "is receiving less than his due" in the United States.

Perhaps the deepest and most critically informed foreign interest in Bierce has been in France. A proposal for a translation during his own lifetime failed—like many others—to come to fruition. In the 1920s, however, some of his work was translated in France, where it was a *succès d'estime*, if not widely popular. With the publication of *Au cœur de la vie* (a translation of *In the Midst of Life* by Jacques Papy) in 1947, however, Bierce's Gallic reputation emerged from the underground. Since that time, he has had increasing recognition in France. Papy followed his initial translation with *Le Dictionnaire du Diable* (*The Devil's Dictionary*), with a preface by Jean Cocteau, in 1955; and *Histoires Impossibles* (drawn largely from *Can Such Things Be?* and *The Parenticide Club*) in 1956, two works which were the basis for the first award (posthumously given) of a new French literary prize—the Prix de l'Humeur Noir—to Bierce. Papy then retranslated the tales of soldiers from *In the Midst of Life*, and they were published in 1957 under the title *Morts Violentes.* He continued his translations with *Contes Noirs* and *Fables Fantastiques* (1962).[15]

And Bierce burst into popular view when Robert Hossein produced *Au cœur de la vie* in 1962 as a cinematic triptych written and directed by a young Frenchman, Robert Enrico, including films based on "Chickamauga," "An Occurrence at

Owl Creek Bridge," and "The Mocking-Bird." This movie, when shown at the San Sebastian Festival in 1963, won the Prize for Best Direction (*grand prix de la mise en scène*) and the Critics' Prize; it then crossed the Atlantic for the First New York Film Festival at Lincoln Center on September 11, 1963.

The most famous of Enrico's three short films was "An Occurrence at Owl Creek Bridge" (*La Rivière du Hibou*), starring Roger Jacquet. It was shown independently of the other two, both in France and America, winning the Short Film Grand Prix at the Cannes Film Festival in 1962 and, in an American adaptation by Marcel Ichac and Paul de Roubaix, an Academy Award as the Best Live-Action Short Subject in 1963. On February 28, 1964, it was produced by Rod Serling over Columbia Broadcasting System television in the Twilight Zone Series.[16] "Chickamauga," another item from Enrico's triptych, played at New York's Carnegie Hall Cinema in the spring of 1967, winning high critical praise.[17]

Bierce has also seized the imagination of a famous Russian moviemaker, Sergei Eisenstein. In a long discussion of the creation of artistic effects through montage, he cites Bierce (along with Freud) as having presented examples of the type of wit the movie editor should keep constantly in mind.[18] Though Eisenstein cited an English version of one of the *Fantastic Fables* ("The Inconsolable Widow," quoted in Chapter 12), Bierce has been translated into Russian in a Soviet version illustrated by Vitalii Goriaev, cartoonist for the Moscow humorous weekly *Krokodil.*[19]

The *Fantastic Fables* have also attracted attention in Mexico, where Spanish translations of the following have appeared in a Mexican periodical: "Legislator and Soap," "Atonement," "Saint and Sinner," "A Defective Petition," "The Limit," "A Causeway," "The Crimson Candle," "The Wooden Guns," and "Revelations." In addition, one of the *Fables from "Fun"* (*"El ganso y el hombre"*) and "Mr. Swiddler's Flip-Flap," one of the *Negligible Tales*, have been translated for the same magazine.[20] And Teutonic interest in Bierce has a long history. His work had been translated into German in the 1920s, a dissertation on him was presented at Tübingen in 1951, and a recent collection of his tales published by Diesterwegs Neusprachliche Bibliothek elicited an admiring critical article in *Die Neueren Sprache* in 1963.

IV *Signs of Change*

Nor have American publishers been idle. The twelve-volume Neale edition of the *Collected Works* was recently reprinted by Gordian Press and by Stechert-Hafner. Since this set is crucial to any serious study of Bierce and since it has not been easily available for many years, these reprints may well stimulate further critical investigation. And of course a constant stream of popular-priced editions of Bierce—usually selections from his tales or *The Devil's Dictionary*—flows from the presses. He is, moreover, much favored by publishers of expensive limited editions.

All these straws in the wind are merely indications. What they suggest is that, if Bierce has not been properly appreciated, he has certainly not been neglected. His merit as a writer and as a thinker in many different fields has been known and recognized by a minority of discerning readers both in this country and abroad for almost a century. Why, then, has he not been acclaimed outside this narrow band of *cognoscenti*?

It has been customary to lay the blame on Bierce's shoulders by damning his work with faint praise. However, his lack of widespread acceptance tells more about the history of critical taste than it does about the quality of his output.[21] His independence and versatility have paradoxically argued against him: those who would accept his polished and barbed satire on the plundering plutocrats of America's Gilded Age were annoyed by the vigor with which he attacked the excesses of democracy; those who admired his wit were uninterested in his political essays; those who were drawn by the clinical precision of his tales wanted him to write nothing else. When Edward Bellamy's *Looking Backward* and William Dean Howells' *Traveler from Altruria* and *Through the Eye of the Needle* were popular, Bierce was writing dystopias. And, of course, in the nineteenth and twentieth centuries, the writer who preferred short stories to novels per se has had a built-in handicap so far as securing a large following was concerned.

Clearly much remains to be done in exploring the real contributions of this enigmatic figure to the American cultural heritage. Nevertheless, recent attempts (such as those of the *Times Literary Supplement*, H. Bruce Franklin, Robert A. Wiggins, and Richard O'Connor) to establish Bierce as belonging to traditions which are gaining vogue miss the point. While contemporary literary fashions may make readers of this age more hospitable to Bierce, a just evaluation of his place in the canon of American letters must await a careful and discriminating analysis of his individual writings, an honest attempt to understand the problems he dealt with and the solutions he proposed, and—above all—a willingness to cast aside the shibboleths that have clustered around his name and to make a positive effort to wrench his work free from the matrix of misunderstanding in which it has become imbedded and to deal with it on its own merits.

Obviously much labor, both scholarly and critical, must precede a sophisticated assessment of his position. This sturdy figure, whose underground reputation has steadily grown with the years, is an isolated landmark in the history of American literature, and his work ought to help readers avoid facile generalizations about the period in which he lived. Bierce's significance, not only to American letters but in world literature, is on the verge of a major reevaluation.

His readiness to explore and extend the possibilities of literature made him an original writer of great versatility. His ability to select the significant incident, his skill at conveying in brief compass the pattern of an entire life, and his extraordinary insight into moments of crisis place his best tales at or very near the pinnacle of the demanding form of the short story.

His view of man and the universe was expressed with rigorous honesty and matchless precision. Bierce was not afraid to follow his intelligence where it led him, and he mastered techniques for transmitting what he saw. The vision was terrifying: searing conflicts at the depths of the human psyche and festering sores on the body politic. Nevertheless, he portrayed that vision with fidelity and clarity, tempered only by wit or irony. The picture he painted—in short stories, essays, letters, satirical verses, and highly compressed short forms—is unclouded by sentimentality or even by sentiment. His view is painfully unflattering, frequently tragic, and often violent.

Yet, in a fundamental sense, Bierce was a humanist: what he gives us is an understanding of our own souls. When conventional props give way, as they now threaten to do, the discerning reader can turn to Ambrose Bierce for solace. He will find no facile optimism, no rosy conviction of the inevitability of progress. But he does find valor and wisdom. Man and the society he has created may go down in defeat, but he can face the wreckage with compassion, honor, and a recognition of the unexercised power of human reason—fragments shored against his ruins.

I add my voice to Lawrence Berkove's in approving Carey McWilliams' perceptive judgment: Bierce's "greatest appeal, perhaps, will always be to those who have been forced, as he was forced, to learn to stand alone and who feel, therefore, the tonic contagion of his spirit, his wit, his stoicism, and his courage."[22] If tragedy and pain cannot be avoided, they can be confronted bravely, endured with dignity and magnanimity. And, if men have not yet learned to use reason in coping with life's problems, they can, with Bierce, respect its distinctive potentialities, even when they are swayed by conformity, bias, or passion.

Notes and References

Preface

1. Carey McWilliams, Introduction to Bierce's *The Devil's Dictionary* (New York, 1957), pp. vi, x-xi.

Chapter One

1. Paul Fatout, *Ambrose Bierce, The Devil's Lexicographer* (Norman, Oklahoma; 1951), p. 25.
2. Bierce to Sergeant Abe Dills, August 13, 1887, published in *Fourth Reunion of the 9th Regiment, Indiana Vet. Vol. Infantry Association, Held at Delphi, Indiana, August 24th and 25th, 1887* (Watseka Republican Book Print), pp. 66-67.
3. *Second Reunion of the Ninth Regiment Indiana Vet. Vol. Infantry Association, Held at Logansport, Ind., August 26th and 27th, 1885* (Watseka Republican Book Print), pp. 60-61.
4. *Ninth Indiana Veteran Volunteer Infantry Association, Proceedings of the Eighteenth Annual Reunion, Logansport, Indiana, October 7-8, 1904*; republished in *Battlefields and Ghosts* ([Palo Alto, California]; 1931), pp. 16-17. See also "On a Mountain," *Collected Works*, I, 225-33; and "The Mocking-Bird," II, 218-29 (*San Francisco Examiner*, May 31, 1891). *Collected Works* are hereafter cited in text and in notes as *Works*.
5. "What I Saw of Shiloh," *Works*, I, 239, 244-45. Appeared in *Examiner*, June 19, 1898, "revised and partly rewritten" from an account "published several years ago in a local weekly."
6. "An Affair of Outposts," *Works*, II, 150 (Christmas *Examiner*, 1897).
7. "War Topics," *Examiner*, June 5, 1898.
8. Fatout, *Devil's Lexicographer*, p. 149.
9. "War Topics," *Examiner*, July 3, 1898.
10. *Works*, II, 46-57. See also Bierce's account "A Little of Chickamauga," *Works*, I, 270-78 ("Chickamauga," *Examiner*, April 24, 1898).
11. Mark M. Boatner, III, *The Civil War Dictionary* (New York, 1959), p. 147.
12. "The Crime at Pickett's Mill," *Works*, I, 279-96.
13. Carey McWilliams, "Ambrose Bierce and His First Love," *Bookman*, LXXV (June, 1932).
14. "The Major's Tale," *Works*, VIII, 65, 71-72. See also "A Sole Survivor," *Works*, I, 385-86.
15. "War Topics," *San Francisco Examiner*, June 5, 1898.

170

Chapter Two

1. " 'Way Down in Alabam'," *Works*, I, 328-48.
2. Boatner, *op. cit.*, p. 946.
3. In the Barrett Collection; the passages quoted are all taken from this notebook.
4. "Across the Plains," "The Mirage," and "A Sole Survivor," *Works*, I, 360-69, 370-80, 387-88.
5. National Archives.
6. *Ibid.*
7. Letter from Emory M. Long to Carey McWilliams, May 15, 1929, Bierce Collection, University of California at Los Angeles.
8. Letter from Bierce to Ruth Robertson, November 3, 1912, *Four Ambrose Bierce Letters*.
9. Fatout, *Devil's Lexicographer*, p. 55.
10. Stanley T. Williams, "Ambrose Bierce and Bret Harte," *American Literature*, XVII (May, 1945), 179-80.
11. *Overland Monthly*, VI (June, 1871), 566.
12. *Ibid.*, pp. 564-65.
13. *Ibid.* (April, 1871), pp. 378, 383.
14. Unpublished letter, Bierce to Bartlett, [June, 1871], Huntington Library, HM 7793.
15. Cecil Y. Lang, ed., *The Swinburne Letters* (New Haven, 1959), II, 144-45.

Chapter Three

Except where otherwise indicated, this chapter is adapted from two articles of mine: "Ambrose Bierce and Charles Warren Stoddard: Some Unpublished Correspondence," *Huntington Library Quarterly*, XXIII (May, 1960), 261-92; and "Ambrose Bierce, John Camden Hotten, *The Fiend's Delight*, and *Nuggets and Dust*," *Huntington Library Quarterly*, XXVIII (August, 1965), 353-71. I am grateful to the editor of *The Huntington Library Quarterly* for permission to use this material. Detailed bibliographical notes are found in these articles.

1. "Prattle," *Argonaut*, III (November 9, 1878), p. 9, col. 3.
2. Bierce to Samuel Loveman, August 5, 1909, *Twenty-One Letters*, p. 13.
3. "Prattle," *Argonaut*, II (February 9, 1878), 9; republished in "Civilization," *Works*, XI, 54-55. Cf. Pascal: "Thought makes the whole dignity of man; therefore endeavor to think well, that is the only morality."
4. "Prattle," *Argonaut*, II (February 9, 1878), 9; republished in "Civilization," *Works*, XI, 57.

172   AMBROSE BIERCE

5. For Hotten as pornographer, see Steven Marcus, *The Other Victorians—A Study of Sexuality and Pornography in Mid-Nineteenth-Century England* (New York, 1964), pp. 67-73.

6. Unpublished letter, Bierce to Amy Wells, September 11, 1893, Bancroft Library.

7. Unpublished letter, Bierce to Silas Orrin Howes, May 12, 1897, Huntington Library, HM 10123.

8. "That Ghost of Mine," *Argonaut*, II (April 6, 1878), p. 6, cols. 2-3.

9. "A Sole Survivor," *Works*, I, 397-400.

Chapter Four

1. Typed copy, University of California at Los Angeles Library.

2. *Ibid.*

3. Ernest J. Hopkins, Introduction to *The Enlarged Devil's Dictionary by Ambrose Bierce* (Garden City, New York; 1967), pp. xix-xx.

4. "A Sole Survivor," *Works*, I, 396-97.

5. Paul Fatout, *Ambrose Bierce and the Black Hills* (Norman, Oklahoma; 1956), pp. 102-103. Readers interested in a fuller account of this phase of Bierce's career are urged to read this absorbing, well-documented book.

6. *Ibid.*, p. 100.

7. *Ibid.*, p. 161.

8. *Ibid.*, p. 4.

9. *Ibid.*, p. 50.

10. Unpublished letters, Bierce to Steele, Barrett Collection.

Chapter Five

1. Unpublished letter, Bierce to Percival Pollard, January 8, 1899, Berg Collection.

2. Unpublished letter, Bierce to Walter Neale, November 6, 1912, Huntington Library, HM 10429.

3. "A Thumb-Nail Sketch," *Works*, XII, 305.

4. Fatout, *Devil's Lexicographer*, p. 223; John F. Stover, *American Railroads* (Chicago, 1961), p. 92.

5. "That Was New York: Town Topics—1," *The New Yorker*, August 14, 1965, pp. 43-44.

6. Unpublished letter, Bierce to Myles Walsh, September 26, 1897, University of Cincinnati.

7. Unpublished letters, Bierce to Carroll Carrington, [December 12?], 1897, Barrett Collection; and to W. C. Morrow, December 23, 1897, Bancroft Library.

8. *Examiner*, March 17, 1895; quoted in McWilliams, *Ambrose Bierce, A Biography* (New York, 1929), pp. 247-48.

9. Quoted in Fatout, "Ambrose Bierce Writes about War," Book Club of California *Quarterly News Letter*, XVI (Fall, 1951), 77.

10. *Examiner*, July 31, 1898; quoted in McWilliams, *Biography*, p. 248.

11. Quoted in Fatout, "Ambrose Bierce Writes about War," pp. 78, 79.

12. Unpublished letter, Andrew Chatto to Bierce, January 21, 1892, Stanford University Libraries, Division of Special Collections, M-2085.

13. Agreement in the Barrett Collection.

14. Bierce's copy of his letter to Danziger, February 1, 1893, Barrett Collection.

15. Frank Monaghan, "Ambrose Bierce and the Authorship of *The Monk and the Hangman's Daughter*," *American Literature*, II (January, 1931), 347-48.

16. Unpublished letter, Harte to Bierce, August 17, 1892, Stanford M-2113.

17. Unpublished letter, Bierce to Stone and Kimball, December 4, 1893, Harvard University.

18. Bierce to Blanche Partington, April 18, 1893, Pope, *Letters*, p. 32; Bierce to Percival Pollard, July 20, 1893, George N. Kummer, "Percival Pollard: Precursor of the 'twenties,'" unpublished doctoral dissertation, New York University, 1947, p. 38.

19. Unpublished letter, Bierce to Miriam Gallison, December 4, 1895, Barrett Collection.

20. Unpublished letter, Gertrude Atherton to Bierce, [September 24, 1890], Pforzheimer Misc. MSS, 1733.

21. Kummer, *op. cit.*, pp. 51-52.

22. Unpublished letter, Bierce to Pollard, May 25, 1896, Berg Collection.

23. Unpublished letter, Bierce to Silas Howes, November 29, 1899, Huntington Library, HM 10126.

Chapter Six

1. Pope, *Letters*, p. 110.

2. *Ibid.*, [April 25, 1912], p. 185.

3. Unpublished letter to Amy Wells, July 10, 1913, Bancroft Library.

4. Bierce to Lora Bierce, November 29, 1910, Pope, *Letters*, p. 166.

5. Bierce to Samuel Loveman, November 27, 1910, *Twenty-One Letters*, p. 21.

6. Bierce to Helen Bierce, January 27, 1913, M. E. Grenander, "Seven Ambrose Bierce Letters," *The Yale University Library Gazette*, XXXII (July, 1957), 15.

7. Unpublished letter, Bierce to Amy Wells, August 16, 1913, Bancroft Library.

8. Bierce to Nellie Sickler, September 21, 1913, [Carey McWilliams, editor], "A Collection of Bierce Letters," *University of California Chronicle*, XXXIV (January, 1932), 48.

Chapter Seven

1. Bierce to George Sterling, February 21, 1907, Pope, *Letters*, p. 131.

Chapter Eight

1. R. S. Crane, *The Languages of Criticism and the Structure of Poetry* (Toronto, 1953), pp. 175-76, 197 (footnote 57).

2. Transferred to III, *Can Such Things Be?* 279-307, for the *Works*. Originally collected in *Tales of Soldiers and Civilians* (1892) and *In the Midst of Life* (1892, 1898).

3. *Works*, VIII, 371.

4. "The Secret of Happiness," *Works*, VI, 305.

5. For example, Bierce to Theresa Wright, June 7, 1901, Carey McWilliams, "New Letters of Ambrose Bierce," *Opinion*, II (May, 1930), 4. See also General Clavering's statement quoted in the analysis of "Parker Adderson, Philosopher": "Death . . . is . . . a loss of such happiness as we have, and of opportunities for more."

6. *Works*, VIII, 351, 370.

7. Unpublished letter, Bierce to Percival Pollard, July 29, 1911, Berg Collection. See also *San Francisco Examiner*, January 28, 1900; and letters to George Sterling, July 11, 1908, and January 29, 1910, Pope, *Letters*, pp. 146, 158.

8. *Works*, II, *In the Midst of Life*, 133-45. Appeared originally as "James Adderson, Philosopher and Wit," *Examiner*, February 22, 1891.

9. See, for example, his Epigram, *Works*, VIII, 347:

> "I think," says the philosopher divine,
> "Therefore I am." Sir, here's a surer sign:
> We know we live, for with our every breath
> We feel the fear and imminence of death.

10. "John Mortonson's Funeral," first collected in *Can Such Things Be?* for the *Works*, Vol. III.

11. January 12, 1901, Adolphe de Castro, *Portrait of Ambrose Bierce* (New York, 1929), p. 293.

12. Transferred to *Works*, II, *In the Midst of Life*, 266-80. Originally appeared in *Argonaut*, October 26, 1878, p. 4. Collected in *Can Such Things Be?* (1893, 1903).

13. Lawrence Berkove, "Ambrose Bierce's Concern with Mind and Man," unpublished dissertation, University of Pennsylvania, 1962, p. 40.

14. Nathaniel Hawthorne, Preface to *The House of the Seven Gables.*

Chapter Nine

1. All these distinctions are modified in order to make them applicable to the short story from certain broad principles developed by R. S. Crane in *Critics and Criticism, Ancient and Modern* (Chicago, 1952), pp. 620-22; and in *The Languages of Criticism, op. cit.*, pp. 162-63, 175-76.

2. I have analyzed these stories in greater detail in an article, "Bierce's Turn of the Screw: Tales of Ironical Terror," *The Western Humanities Review*, XI (Summer, 1957), 257-64. I acknowledge with thanks permission granted by the editors of this publication to condense this material here. "One of the Missing" (*Examiner*, March 11, 1888), "Chickamauga" (*Examiner*, January 20, 1889, p. 9), "An Occurrence at Owl Creek Bridge" (*Examiner*, July 13, 1890, p. 12), and "The Man and the Snake" (*Examiner*, June 29, 1890) appeared in *Tales of Soldiers and Civilians* (1892), *In the Midst of Life* (1892, 1898), and Vol. II of the *Works*, *In the Midst of Life*. "One Officer, One Man" ("A Coward," *Examiner*, February 17, 1889) was collected in *Can Such Things Be?* (1893, 1903), but was transferred to *Works*, Vol. II (*In the Midst of Life*).

3. Criticism makes strange bedfellows. This story was much admired by both James Whitcomb Riley and Stephen Crane. See Will H. Thompson to Bierce, unpublished letter, June 15, 1906, Stanford M-2323; and Stephen Crane to Richard Harding Davis, *Stephen Crane: Letters*, ed. R. W. Stallman and Lillian Gilkes (New York, 1960), pp. 139-40, n. 94.

4. Berkove, *op. cit.*, pp. 149-56.

5. *Works*, III, *Can Such Things Be?* 174-84. Not in the earlier editions of *Can Such Things Be?*

6. Transferred to *Works*, III, *Can Such Things Be?* 106-20. Originally published in the *Examiner*, September 30, 1888, p. 9. Collected in *Tales of Soldiers and Civilians* (1892) and *In the Midst of Life* (1892, 1898).

7. *Works*, III, *Can Such Things Be?* 13-43. Collected in 1893 and 1903 editions. Originally published in Christmas *Wave*, 1891.

8. "My Favorite Murder," *The Parenticide Club*, *Works*, VIII, 160.

9. A similar epigraph from "Hali" precedes "An Inhabitant of Carcosa," first collected in *Can Such Things Be?* for the *Works*, Vol. III.

10. "The Realm of the Unreal," *Works*, III, 262-63.

11. " 'On with the Dance!'—A Review," *Works*, VIII, 267-68.

12. See his essay, "Visions of the Night," *Works*, X, 122-33.

Chapter Ten

1. "Columbus," *Works*, IX, *Tangential Views*, 71.

2. *Works*, II, *In the Midst of Life*, 105-21. Originally published in the *Examiner*, October 20, 1889. Collected in *Tales of Soldiers and Civilians* (1892) and *In the Midst of Life* (1892, 1898).

3. *Works*, II, *In the Midst of Life*, 58-70. First published in the *Examiner*, July 29, 1888, p. 9. Collected in *Tales of Soldiers and Civilians* (1892) and *In the Midst of Life* (1892, 1898).

4. "What I Saw of Shiloh," *Works*, I, 257.

5. *The Wasp*, July 14, 1883; quoted in McWilliams, *Biography*, p. 45.

6. *Works*, II, *In the Midst of Life*, [15]-26. Originally published as "The Horseman in the Sky," *Examiner*, April 14, 1889. Collected in *Tales of Soldiers and Civilians* (1892) and *In the Midst of Life* (1892, 1898).

7. See Guy A. Cardwell, "The Duel in the Old South: Crux of a Concept," *The South Atlantic Quarterly*, LXVI (Winter, 1967), 50-69.

8. Berkove, *op. cit.*, pp. 143-49.

9. Bierce, Introduction to Josephine Clifford McCrackin's *The Woman Who Lost Him and Tales of the Army Frontier* (Pasadena, California; 1913), p. [v]. Berkove also quotes this passage, *op. cit.*, p. 127.

10. Berkove, *op. cit.*, p. 87.

11. Martin Russ, *The Last Parallel—A Marine's War Journal* (New York, 1957), p. 307. Significantly, Russ refers to Bierce on p. 309.

Chapter Eleven

1. Transferred to *Works*, VIII, *Negligible Tales*, 23-40. First collected in *Can Such Things Be?* (1893, 1903).

2. William McCann, *Ambrose Bierce's Civil War* (Chicago, 1956), pp. 247-57. McCann has also silently eliminated the account of a Confederate general, Schneddeker Baumschank.

3. Bierce was born near Horse Cave Creek, Ohio.

4. *Works*, II, *In the Midst of Life*, 290-310. Collected in *Tales of Soldiers and Civilians* (1892) and *In the Midst of Life* (1892, 1898). Appeared originally as "The Watcher by the Dead," *Examiner*, December 29, 1889.

5. "The Chair of Little Ease," *Works*, XI, *Antepenultimata*, 366.

6. In *Works*, XI, *Antepenultima ta*, 328-33.

7. All in *Can Such Things Be? Works*, Vol. III.

8. *Works*, II, *In the Midst of Life*, 350-63. Collected in *Tales of Soldiers and Civilians* (1892) and *In the Midst of Life* (1892, 1898). Appeared originally in the *Examiner*, July 14, 1889.

9. Berkove, *op. cit.*, pp. 121-23.

Chapter Twelve

1. Unpublished letter, Bierce to Neale, October 25, 1909, Huntington Library, HM 10262.

2. Preface to *Works*, IV, *Shapes of Clay*, [9].

3. Preface, WIT, and WITTICISM, *Works*, Vol. VII, *The Devil's Dictionary*; "Wit and Humor," X, 99-101; *Epigrams*, VIII, 346; "Word Changes and Slang," X, 107. See also "The Matter of Manner," X, 62.

4. See *Write It Right*, Preface and p. 5; "The Matter of Manner," *Works*, X, 57-64; "Taking Oneself Off," *Works*, XI, *Antepenultima ta*, 341-42; and the definitions of LEXICOGRAPHER and OBSOLETE in *Works*, Vol. VII, *The Devil's Dictionary*.

5. *Write It Right*, p. 7.

6. The reader is directed also to a relatively long and serious essay, "Some Features of the Law," *Works*, XI, 99-129; and to a satirical verse addressed to Hall McAllister, "To an Insolent Attorney," *Works*, V, *Black Beetles in Amber*, 240-42.

7. *Fantastic Fables, Works*, VI, 234; see also VI, "A Hasty Settlement" (184-85); "The Party Over There" (194-95); "The Tried Assassin" (203); "The No Case" (230); "An Unspeakable Imbecile" (248); "A Fatal Disorder" (273-74); "The Justice and His Accuser" (276-77); "Snake and Swallow" (347); and "Lion and Mouse" ([363]-364).

8. *Fantastic Fables, Works*, VI, 268-69.

9. *Ibid.*, p. 294.

10. *The Scrap Heap, Works*, IV, 361.

11. *Epigrams, Works*, VIII, 365.

12. *Ibid.*

13. *Write It Right*, p. 40.

14. *Works*, Vol. VII. See also the entries under BELLADONNA, HELPMATE, HUSBAND, INDISCRETION, LOVE, MAIDEN, MISS, MOUTH, OPPOSE, POLYGAMY, REFUSAL, SEINE, SIREN, SUFFRAGE, UGLINESS, UXORIOUSNESS, WEAKNESSES, WEDDING, WITCH, WOMAN, and YOKE.

15. *Fantastic Fables, Works*, VI, 204.

16. *Ibid.*, p. 311.

17. See, for example, in addition to "The Inconsolable Widow," quoted above, "Privation" in *Works*, V, *Black Beetles in Amber*, 301-302.

18. *Epigrams, Works*, VIII, 353.

19. *Ibid.*, p. 377; also in *The Scrap Heap, Works*, IV, 362.

20. See, for example, his letters to Dr. Doyle, January 23, 1901, and to George Sterling, February 18, 1905, Pope, *Letters*, pp. 42-44, 105; " 'On with the Dance!'—A Review," *Works*, VIII, 267-68, 288; "Cows," *Works*, XII, 173-74; "The Realm of the Unreal," *Works*, III, 262-63.

21. Sergei Eisenstein, *The Film Sense*, ed. and trans. by Jay Leyda (New York, 1957; bound with *Film Form*), pp. 4-7.

Chapter Thirteen

1. Robert E. Spiller, Willard Thorp, Thomas H. Johnson, Henry Seidel Canby, editors, *Literary History of the United States* (New York, 1953), pp. 1068-70.

2. Emily Hahn, *Romantic Rebels* (Boston, 1967), *passim.*

3. McWilliams, Introduction to *The Devil's Dictionary*, pp. vi, x.

4. *The Works of Stephen Crane*, ed. Wilson Follett (New York, 1926), VII, xiii, xv.

5. Daniel G. Hoffman, *The Poetry of Stephen Crane* (New York, 1957), *passim*; R. W. Stallman, *Stephen Crane: An Omnibus* (New York, 1952), pp. 568-69.

6. See, for example, Philip Young, *Ernest Hemingway: A Reconsideration* (University Park, Fla.; 1966), pp. 197-98; and John Kenney Crane, "Crossing the Bar Twice: Post-Mortem Consciousness in Bierce, Hemingway, and Golding," *Studies in Short Fiction*, VI (Summer, 1969), 361-76.

7. *Letters of James Agee to Father Flye*, ed. James Harold Flye (New York, 1962), pp. 96-97. I am grateful to my colleague Theodore Adams for bringing this letter to my attention.

8. Walford Davies, "Imitation and Invention: the Use of Borrowed Material in Dylan Thomas's Prose," *Essays in Criticism*, XVII (July, 1968), 275-95.

9. H. Bruce Franklin, *Future Perfect—American Science Fiction of the Nineteenth Century* (New York, 1966), pp. 268-70, 378.

10. Thomas Paine, *Common Sense, Thomas Paine's Political Writings*, ed. Nelson F. Adkins (New York, 1953), p. 4. Consider also the optimistic suggestions in the first and last paragraphs of Thoreau's *Civil Disobedience.*

11. Harold D. Lasswell and Abraham Kaplan, *Power and Society: A Framework for Political Inquiry* (New Haven, 1950), pp. 279-80. Bierce's definition of REVOLUTION is from *Works*, VII, *The Devil's Dictionary*, 292. The other quotations illustrating his views on political science have all been taken from the following essays in *Works*, XI, *Antepenultimata*: "The Shadow on the Dial," 15-48; "Civilization,"

49-64; and "The American Sycophant," 296-309. See also Fatout, *Devil's Lexicographer*, pp. 207-208. The dystopias cited are found in *Works*, I, *Ashes of the Beacon*, 17-222, and in XII, *In Motley*, 343-55.

12. Van Wyck Brooks, "The Letters of Ambrose Bierce," *Emerson and Others* (New York, 1927), pp. 147-57. Gordian Press has reprinted the Pope *Letters*, the volume reviewed by Brooks in his essay.

13. Eric Partridge, "Ambrose Bierce," *London Mercury*, XVI (October, 1927), 630.

14. *American Writing Today: Its Independence and Vigor*, ed. Allan Angoff (New York, 1957), pp. 58-65, 182.

15. Robert Coiplet, "Histoires impossibles d'Ambrose Bierce," *Le Monde*, 19 mai 1956, p. 8; "Bierce's French Prize," *Christian Science Monitor*, October 4, 1956. I am grateful to Roger Asselineau, Professor of American Literature at the Sorbonne and Visiting Distinguished Professor of English at SUNYA in the spring semester of 1968, for supplying me with some of the Papy translations.

16. *Who's Who in France; Contemporary Films, Inc., Supplement No. 2* (New York), p. 74; Arthur Schlesinger, Jr., "Film as Myth: The Western," *Show*, III (April, 1963), 38; *Saturday Review*, October 5, 1963, p. 68. I am also indebted to two of my colleagues, James M. Leonard and Frederick E. Silva, for information on cinematic adaptations of Bierce.

17. Brendan Gill, "The Current Cinema," *The New Yorker*, April 1, 1967, pp. 94-95.

18. Eisenstein, *op. cit.*, pp. 4-7.

19. Winsted (Connecticut) *Citizen*, May 27, 1958.

20. All these appeared in *El Cuento*, No. 13 (June, 1965), pp. 498-500; and Nos. 9-10 (January-February, 1965), pp. 32-34. I am grateful to Mrs. Elnora Carrino for supplying me with these translations.

21. In this connection, see Michael Zimmerman, "Literary Revivalism in America: Some Notes Toward a Hypothesis," *American Quarterly*, XIX (Spring, 1967), 71-85.

22. McWilliams, Introduction to *Devil's Dictionary*, pp. xi-xii; quoted by Berkove, *op. cit.*, p. 7, f.n. 24.

Selected Bibliography

PRIMARY SOURCES

I have made no attempt to list Bierce's contributions to periodicals; see the bibliographies.

1. *Books by Bierce* (Chronologically arranged)

Dod Grile [Ambrose Bierce]. *The Fiend's Delight.* London: John Camden Hotten, [1873].

————. *Nuggets and Dust.* London: Chatto and Windus, [1873].

————. *Cobwebs from an Empty Skull.* London: George Routledge and Sons, 1874.

William Herman [Ambrose Bierce and T. A. Harcourt]. *The Dance of Death.* San Francisco: Henry Keller & Co., 1877.

Dod Grile [Ambrose Bierce]. *Cobwebs.* London: *Fun* Office, ca. 1884. (A reissue of *Cobwebs from an Empty Skull.*)

Ambrose Bierce. *Tales of Soldiers and Civilians.* San Francisco: E. L. G. Steele, [1892, not 1891 as on title page].

————. *In the Midst of Life—Tales of Soldiers and Civilians.* London: Chatto and Windus, 1892.

Ambrose Bierce and Gustav Adolph Danziger. *The Monk and the Hangman's Daughter.* Chicago: F. J. Schulte and Company, 1892.

Ambrose Bierce. *Black Beetles in Amber.* San Francisco: Western Authors Publishing Company, 1892.

————. *Can Such Things Be?* New York: The Cassell Publishing Company, 1893.

————. *In the Midst of Life—Tales of Soldiers and Civilians.* New York: G. P. Putnam's Sons, 1898.

————. *Fantastic Fables.* New York: G. P. Putnam's Sons, 1899.

————. *Shapes of Clay.* San Francisco: W. E. Wood, 1903.

————. *The Cynic's Word Book.* New York: Doubleday, Page & Company, 1906.

————. *A Son of the Gods and A Horseman in the Sky.* Introduction by W. C. Morrow. San Francisco: Paul Elder and Company, 1907.

Ambrose Bierce and G. A. Danziger. *The Monk and the Hangman's Daughter.* New York and Washington: The Neale Publishing Company, 1907. Important for the copyright notices (1891, 1903, and 1907) and for Bierce's Preface paying tribute to Richard Voss, the original author.

Ambrose Bierce. *Write It Right*. New York and Washington: The Neale Publishing Company, 1909. Not in *Collected Works*.

————. *The Shadow on the Dial and Other Essays*. Ed. S. O. Howes. San Francisco: A. M. Robertson, 1909.

The Collected Works of Ambrose Bierce. New York and Washington: The Neale Publishing Company, 1909-12. 12 Vols. Cited throughout this study as *Works*.

Selections from Prattle by Ambrose Bierce. Ed. Carroll D. Hall. San Francisco: The Book Club of California, 1936.

The Collected Writings of Ambrose Bierce. Ed. Clifton Fadiman. New York: The Citadel Press, 1946. Best modern one-volume selection (the title is a misnomer) from Bierce's *Works*.

The Enlarged Devil's Dictionary of Ambrose Bierce. Ed. Ernest J. Hopkins. Garden City, New York: Doubleday & Company, 1967. Resurrects many entries from Bierce's periodical writings not included in the *Works*. The introduction, however, is not completely reliable.

2. Bibliographies

Blanck, Joseph. "Ambrose Gwinnett Bierce, 1842-1914(?)," *Bibliography of American Literature*. New Haven: Yale University Press, 1955. I, 216-27.

Fatout, Paul. "Ambrose Bierce (1842-1914)," *American Literary Realism, 1870-1910*, I (Fall, 1967), 13-19.

Gaer, Joseph, ed. *Ambrose Gwinett [sic] Bierce, Bibliography and Biographical Data*. California Literary Research, Monograph No. 4 from SERA Project 2-F2-132 (3-F2-197). California Relief Administration: 1935. Mimeographed. Reprinted by Burt Franklin, Publisher, in 1968.

Grenander, M. E. "*Au cœur de la vie*: A French Translation of Ambrose Bierce," *Boston University Studies in English*, I (Winter, 1955-56), 237-41.

————. "Ambrose Bierce, John Camden Hotten, *The Fiend's Delight*, and *Nuggets and Dust*," *Huntington Library Quarterly*, XXVIII (August, 1965), 353-71.

Starrett, Vincent. *Ambrose Bierce, A Bibliography*. Philadelphia: The Centaur Book Shop, 1929.

3. Published Letters

Chittick, V. L. O. "Holograph Treasures in the Reed College Library Adams Collection, III," *Reed College Notes*, IX (April, 1947).

Containing Four Ambrose Bierce Letters. [New York: Charles Romm, 1923.] A manila envelope containing four printed letters, each on a single leaf.

Grenander, M. E. "Ambrose Bierce and Charles Warren Stoddard: Some Unpublished Correspondence," *Huntington Library Quarterly*, XXIII (May, 1960), 261-92.

————. "H. L. Mencken to Ambrose Bierce," The Book Club of California *Quarterly News Letter*, XXII (Winter, 1956), 5-10.

————. "Seven Ambrose Bierce Letters," *The Yale University Library Gazette*, XXXII (July, 1957), 12-18.

Jackson, Hartley E. and James D. Hart. *Battlefields and Ghosts*. [Palo Alto, California]: The Harvest Press, 1931. Appeared originally as a paper enclosed with a letter from Bierce to Alex. Whitehall, October 1, 1904, in *Ninth Indiana Veteran Volunteer Infantry Association, Proceedings of the Eighteenth Annual Reunion, Logansport, Indiana, October 7-8, 1904*.

Loveman, Samuel, ed. *Twenty-one Letters of Ambrose Bierce*. Cleveland: George Kirk, 1922.

[McWilliams, Carey.] "A Collection of Bierce Letters," *University of California Chronicle*, XXXIV (January, 1932), 30-48.

McWilliams, Carey. "Ambrose Bierce and His First Love," *The Bookman* (New York), LXXV (June, 1932), 254-59.

————. "New Letters of Ambrose Bierce," *Opinion*, II (May, 1930), 3-4.

Pope, Bertha Clark, ed. *The Letters of Ambrose Bierce*. San Francisco: The Book Club of California, 1922. Reprinted by Gordian Press in 1967.

Ridgely, J. V. "Ambrose Bierce to H. L. Mencken," The Book Club of California *Quarterly News Letter*, XXVI (Fall, 1961), 27-33.

Williams, Stanley T. "Ambrose Bierce and Bret Harte," *American Literature*, XVII (May, 1945), 179-80.

4. *Manuscript Materials*

Bancroft Library of the University of California at Berkeley.
Barrett Collection, the Clifton Waller; now at the University of Virginia.
Boston Public Library.
California Historical Society.
California State Library.
California, University of, at Los Angeles; Department of Special Collections.
Cincinnati, University of.
Columbia University, Special Collections.
Dartmouth College.
Driscoll, Michael B.
Goldstone, M. B.
Hart, James D.
Harvard University.

Huntington Library, San Marino, California.
Library of Congress.
Marchand, Ernest.
Mills College.
Mordell, Albert.
Morgan Library, The J. Pierpont.
National Archives.
New York Public Library, The: Berg Collection, Anthony Collection,
    Century Collection, Merle Johnson, Miscellaneous.
Oakland Public Library, California Room.
Pennsylvania, University of.
Perrin, Alfred H.
Pforzheimer Library, The Carl H.
Pollard, Joseph P., Jr.
Princeton University.
St. John's Seminary, Camarillo, California.
San Francisco Public Library.
Seelig, George R.
Society of California Pioneers.
Southern California, University of; American Literature Collection.
Stanford University Libraries, The Division of Special Collections.
Suman, Mrs. A. L.
Texas, University of.
Tufts, Dr. John M.
Wagner College.
Yale University Library, Collection of American Literature.

SECONDARY SOURCES

Bahr, Howard W. "Ambrose Bierce and Realism," *The Southern Quart-
    erly*, I (July, 1963), 309-31. Excellent critical interpretation.
Berkove, Lawrence. "Ambrose Bierce's Concern with Mind and Man."
    Unpublished doctoral dissertation, Pennsylvania, 1962. One of the
    few really useful full-length studies.
Bishop, Morris. "The Mystery of Ambrose Bierce," *The New Yorker*,
    February 26, 1949. Wittiest of the many fictional treatments of
    Bierce's disappearance.
Boynton, Percy Holmes. *More Contemporary Americans*. Chicago: The
    University of Chicago Press, 1927. Surveys not only Bierce's short
    stories but also his other work; comments on his political and social
    theories.

Brooks, Van Wyck. *Emerson and Others*. New York: E. P. Dutton and Company, 1927. "The Letters of Ambrose Bierce" is a perceptive study of Bierce's character based on his letters.

————. *The Confident Years: 1885-1915*. [New York]: E. P. Dutton & Co., Inc., 1952. Chapter XI, "San Francisco: Ambrose Bierce," repeats the well-worn errors of earlier studies. Asserts that the character Boscowitz in Josiah Royce's novel, *The Feud of Ashfield Creek* (Boston: Houghton, Mifflin & Company, 1887), was modeled on Bierce. If so, it is a misleading interpretation.

Cooper, Frederick Tabor. *Some American Story Tellers*. New York: Henry Holt and Company, 1911. Includes essay which presents Bierce "under three separate aspects: the Critic, the Satirist and the Master of the Short Story," and concludes that he is "entitled to hearty recognition as an enduring figure in American letters."

De Castro (formerly Danziger), Adolphe. *Portrait of Ambrose Bierce*. New York: The Century Co., 1929. Unreliable.

Fatout, Paul. *Ambrose Bierce, The Devil's Lexicographer*. Norman: University of Oklahoma Press, 1951. Much useful factual information.

————. "Ambrose Bierce Writes about War," The Book Club of California *Quarterly News Letter*, XVI (Fall, 1951), 75-79. Discusses Bierce's attitude toward Spanish-American War.

————. "Ambrose Bierce, Civil War Topographer," *American Literature*, XXVI (November, 1954), 391-400. Useful information about Bierce's technical assignments in Civil War.

————. *Ambrose Bierce and the Black Hills*. Norman: University of Oklahoma Press, 1956. Almost a model of the kind of biographical investigation now necessary. Based on primary sources, it is a penetrating examination of a critical period which had not been investigated. In this book, his second on Bierce, Fatout has revised some judgments he made in his first.

Follett, Wilson. "Ambrose Bierce—An Analysis of the Perverse Wit that Shaped His Work," *The Bookman* (New York), LXVIII (November, 1928), 284-89. Ingenious dissection of Bierce's short forms.

Grenander, Mary Elizabeth. "The Critical Theories of Ambrose Bierce." Unpublished doctoral dissertation, Chicago, 1948. Discussion of Bierce's esthetic theories.

————. "Bierce's Turn of the Screw: Tales of Ironical Terror," *The Western Humanities Review*, XI (Summer, 1957), 257-63. More extended analysis of the stories discussed in this book in Chapter 9, Section 1.

Hall, Carroll D. *Bierce and the Poe Hoax*. San Francisco: The Book Club of California, 1934. Describes the pretended "discovery" of a purported lost Poe work actually by Herman Scheffauer.

Josephson, Matthew. *Portrait of the Artist as American*. New York:

Octagon Books, Inc., 1964. Reprint of a 1930 study which shows some insight.

Klein, Marcus. "San Francisco and Her Hateful Ambrose Bierce," *The Hudson Review*, VII (Autumn, 1954), 392-407. Provocative discussion marred by erroneous assumptions about Bierce's esthetic theory.

Kummer, George N. "Percival Pollard: Precursor of the 'twenties.' " Unpublished doctoral dissertation, New York University, 1947. Useful account of Pollard's relations with Bierce.

Mahoney, Tom. "The End of Ambrose Bierce," *Esquire*, February, 1936, pp. 62, 149-50. Valuable information about Bierce's disappearance.

McWilliams, Carey. *Ambrose Bierce, A Biography.* New York: Albert & Charles Boni, 1929. One of the earliest full-length studies; still valuable. A second edition was published in 1967 by Archon Books, Hamden, Conn., with an important new Introduction (pp. xi-xxxi).

————. Introduction. Ambrose Bierce, *The Devil's Dictionary*. New York: Sagamore Press Inc., 1957. Brilliant short essay summarizing years of thoughtful study.

Mencken, H. L. *A Book of Prefaces.* New York: Alfred A. Knopf, 1917. Valuable for Mencken's judgment of Bierce, as is the next entry.

————. *Prejudices, Sixth Series.* New York: Alfred A. Knopf, 1927. "Ambrose Bierce," pp. 259-65.

Miller, Arthur M. "The Influence of Edgar Allan Poe on Ambrose Bierce," *American Literature*, IV (May, 1932), 130-50. Questionable.

Monaghan, Frank. "Ambrose Bierce and the Authorship of *The Monk and the Hangman's Daughter*," *American Literature*, II (January, 1931), 337-49. Comparison of the Bierce-Danziger version with Richard Voss's German original.

O'Brien, Robert. "Did Ambrose Bierce Commit Suicide?" Riptides, San Francisco *Chronicle*, February 8, 1950. Conjectures about Bierce's last days.

O'Connor, Richard. *Ambrose Bierce: A Biography.* Boston: Little, Brown and Company, 1967. A "popular" biography, smoothly written but with little new information and some misinformation.

Pira, Gisela. "Ambrose Bierce," *Die Neueren Sprache* (1963), pp. 425-30. Concentrates on "A Horseman in the Sky," "Parker Adderson, Philosopher," and "Killed at Resaca." Despite a few errors of fact, has some critical insights; e. g., "Selbstbeherrschung ist eine Eigenart des Bierceschen Menschen."

Pollard, Percival. *Their Day in Court.* New York: The Neale Publishing Co., 1909. One-sided appraisal by an enthusiastic admirer.

Scheffauer, Herman George. "Ambrose Bierce—ein amerikanischer Satiriker," *Preussische Jahrbücher*, CCV (September, 1926),

329-37. Early indication of German interest in Bierce, written by a quondam "pupil."

Sheller, Harry Lynn. "The Satire of Ambrose Bierce: Its Objects, Forms, Devices, and Possible Origins." Unpublished doctoral dissertation, Southern California, 1945. Extremely valuable study, detailed and scholarly.

Solomon, Eric. "The Bitterness of Battle: Ambrose Bierce's War Fiction," *The Midwest Quarterly*, V, 147-65. Useful.

Sterling, George. "The Shadow Maker," *The American Mercury*, VI (September, 1925), 10-19. Appraisal by a former "pupil."

Walker, Franklin. *Ambrose Bierce: The Wickedest Man in San Francisco*. [San Francisco]: The Colt Press, 1941. Conventional interpretation.

————. *San Francisco's Literary Frontier*. New York: Alfred A. Knopf, Inc., 1939. Valuable study of the local milieu in which Bierce operated during much of his career.

Weimer, David R. "Ambrose Bierce and the Art of War," in *Essays in Literary History*, ed. Rudolf Kirk and C. F. Main. New York: Russell and Russell, 1965. Analyzes seven of the war stories.

Wiggins, Robert A. *Ambrose Bierce*. Minneapolis: University of Minnesota Press, 1964. University of Minnesota Pamphlets on American Writers, No. 37. Short study, not completely reliable.

Wilson, Edmund. *Patriotic Gore: Studies in the Literature of the American Civil War*. New York: Oxford University Press, 1962. "Ambrose Bierce on the Owl Creek Bridge" is a revision of a review in *The New Yorker*, December 8, 1951, of Fatout's *Ambrose Bierce, The Devil's Lexicographer*, which began: "There is as yet no book on Ambrose Bierce that can really be said to come to grips with its prickly and puzzling subject." Yet, when Wilson revised his review to form a chapter in *Patriotic Gore*, he omitted this qualification and leaned heavily on the same sources he had earlier questioned.

Wilt, Napier. "Ambrose Bierce and the Civil War," *American Literature*, I (November, 1929), 260-85. Study based on government documents of Bierce's Civil War career.

Woodruff, Stuart C. *The Short Stories of Ambrose Bierce: A Study in Polarity*. [No city:] University of Pittsburgh Press, 1964. A 1962 Connecticut doctoral dissertation. Oversimplified interpretation of Bierce's stories.

Index

Adams, Theodore, 178
Adriatic, 42
Aerial Steam Navigation Company, 31
Agee, James, 161, 178
Alabama, 20, 24-26; Huntsville, 25; post-Civil War corruption in, 26; Selma, 26-27
Alta California, San Francisco, 34, 38
Ambrose Gwinett; or, A Sea-side Story (Jerrold), 38
American Authors' Guild, 61
American letters, AB's place in, 168
American Publishers Corporation, 59, 61
Ancestry, 15
Angoff, Allan, 179
Argonaut, 46, 51-52, 76, 171, 172, 175
Aristotle, 152, 163
Army, enlistment, 16; rank in, 16-17, 19-20, 28-30; reenlistment, 17; resignation from, 25; topographical engineer in, 20
Army of the Cumberland, 19-24
Army of the Ohio, 17-19
Army of the Tennessee, 17
Arnold, Matthew, 34
Asselineau, Roger, 179
Asthma, 26, 28, 34, 41, 43, 51, 53, 67, 74-75
Atavism, 138, 140-41
Atherton, Gertrude, 42, 62-63, 161, 173
Atlantic, The, 23
Avitor, 31

Bacon, Francis, 32
Balzac, Honoré de, 31
Bancroft, A. L., and Company, 46
Bancroft Library, 172, 173, 174
Barrett Collection, 171, 172, 173
Bartlett, William C., 32-33, 171
Beatty, Brig. Gen. Samuel, 23-24
Bellamy, Edward, 167
Belloc, Hilaire, 63
Berg Collection, 172, 173, 174
Berkove, Lawrence, 92, 96, 128-29, 141, 169, 175, 176, 177, 179
Bible, 53
Bierce, Albert, 16, 21, 23, 43-44, 73

Bierce, Ambrose, writings: "A Causeway," 166; "A Coward," 175; "A Defective Petition," 154, 166; "A Fatal Disorder," 177; "A Hasty Settlement," 177; "A Horseman in the Sky," 55, 115, 123-30; "A Lacking Factor," 115; "A Little of

Chickamauga," 170; "A Matter of Method," 158-59; "A Mystery," 31; "A Resumed Identity," 20, 99-102; "A Sole Survivor," 170, 171, 172; "A Son of the Gods," 55, 115, 119-23; "A Thumb-Nail Sketch," 172; "A Tough Tussle," 55, 99, 102-6, 111, 138, 140; "A Watcher by the Dead," 111, 131, 138-41; "Across the Plains," 171; *Aesopus Emendatus*, 158; "An Affair of Outposts," 18-19, 170; "An Error," 155; "An Imperfect Conflagration," 131-32; "An Inhabitant of Carcosa," 176; "An Occurrence at Owl Creek Bridge," 55, 93-99, 139, 165-66, 175; "An Unspeakable Imbecile," 177; *Antepenultimata*, 69, 149, 178-79; "Ashes of the Beacon," 163; "Atonement," 166; "Basilica," 31; *Battlefields and Ghosts*, 170; "Beyond the Wall," 141; *Black Beetles in Amber*, 60-61, 152, 177; *Can Such Things Be?* 33, 61, 92, 102, 165, 174, 175, 176, 177; "Chickamauga," 21, 55, 65, 93-99, 165-66, 170, 176; "Civilization," 37, 171, 178-79; *Cobwebs from an Empty Skull*, 38; *Cobwebs*, 38; *Collected Works*, [7], 40-41, 68-69, 71, 73, 92, 102, 128, 167; "Columbus," 115, 176; "Cows," 177, 178; "Deceased and Heirs," 154; "Dethronement of the Atom," 152; "Dies Irae," 44; "D.T.," 40; Epigrams, 39-41, 79, 81-82, 88, 110, 119-20, 148-49, 151, 155-57, 174, 177, 178; Fables, 79, 154-56, 158-59; *Fables from "Fun,"* 166; *Fantastic Fables*, 62, 81, 154-56, 158-59, 166, 177; "Female Suffrage," 31; "For the Ahkoond," 163; "George Thurston," 20; Grizzly Papers, 32-33, 40; "Haïta the Shepherd," 80-84; "Hen and Vipers," 158-59; *In Motley*, 69, 164, 179; *In the Midst of Life*, 58, 62, 67, 92, 102, 174, 175, 176, 177; "James Adderson, Philosopher and Wit," 174; "John Bartine's Watch," 141; "John Mortonson's Funeral," 174; "John Smith, Liberator," 163; "Judge and Plantiff," 154; "Jupiter Doke, Brigadier-General," 131-38; "Legislator and Soap," 166; Letters, 76, 81, 161, 164-65, 171, 173, 174, 178, 179; "Lion and

About the Author

Mary Elizabeth Grenander is Professor of English at the State University of New York at Albany, where she has been on the faculty since 1948. Born in Rewey, Wisconsin, she took her A.B. and A.M. degrees from the University of Chicago.

During World War II, from 1942 to 1946, she served in Massachusetts, New York City, and Washington as a Wave in the United States Naval Reserve, being demobilized as a lieutenant. She then returned to Chicago for her Ph.D., which she took in 1948 with a dissertation on Ambrose Bierce.

She has spent one year doing research at the Huntington Library, San Marino, California; one year as Fulbright Visiting Professor of American Literature at the Facultés des Lettres, Lille and Toulouse, France; and one year doing research at the Barrett Collection of the University of Virginia. She has received grants from the Huntington Library, The Pforzheimer Foundation, and the Research Foundation of the State University of New York. A number of her articles on such authors as Donne, Milton, Dickens, and Henry James have been published in *PMLA, American Literature, University of Toronto Quarterly, Nineteenth-Century Fiction*, and other journals.